COP

Valentin Gendrot worked on local newspapers and radio after graduating from journalism college, and carried out several undercover investigations — including working on a Toyota production line and in a Lidl supermarket — before joining the Paris police force.

COP

A JOURNALIST
INFILTRATES THE POLICE

VALENTIN GENDROT
TRANSLATED BY FRANK WYNNE

SCRIBE
Melbourne • London

Scribe Publications
2 John St, Clerkenwell, London, WC1N 2ES, United Kingdom
18–20 Edward St, Brunswick, Victoria 3056, Australia
3754 Pleasant Ave, Suite 100, Minneapolis, Minnesota 55409, USA

Originally published in French by Éditions Goutte d'Or as *Flic* in
2020
Published by Scribe in 2021

Typeset in Adobe Caslon Pro by the publishers

Printed and bound in the UK by CPI Group (UK) Ltd, Croydon
CR0 4YY

Scribe Publications is committed to the sustainable use of natural
resources and the use of paper products made responsibly from those
resources.

978 1 913348 88 5 (UK edition)
978 1 922310 77 4 (Australian edition)
978 1 950354 84 9 (US edition)
978 1 922585 16 5 (ebook)

Catalogue records for this book are available from the National
Library of Australia and the British Library.

scribepublications.co.uk
scribepublications.com.au
scribepublications.com

For my beloved father

For La Merguez

For Marcelo

EDITORS' NOTE

Never has a journalist attempted — and pulled off — such a venture: infiltrating the police. Reporters have gone undercover as labourers on building sites (Günter Wallraff in Germany), and as prison wardens (Ted Conover in the United States, Arthur Frayer in France); others have feigned madness to get access to psychiatric hospitals (Nelly Bly in the United States, Albert Londres in France). In *Cop*, a journalist takes us on an undercover journey to the heart of a French police station.

When the idea fist occurred to him, Valentin Gendrot was twenty-nine, and had already racked up six stints as an undercover reporter. He had just come out of a three-year period during which he had gone undercover in various professions: as a production-line worker in a car factory, a door-to-door salesman, and a call-centre worker. From this research, he wrote his first book under the pseudonym Thomas Morel, entitled *The Enslaved: a year spent with zero-hours underpaid workers* (Les Arènes, 2017).

Why, this time, did he decide to infiltrate the police? First, because it was a personal challenge: to be the first journalist to make the attempt. Second, to satisfy the desire to answer a number of crucial questions.

What happens behind the closed doors of a police station? How has police brutality come to be a recurring theme? Are the French police bigoted and institutionally racist? Why is it so difficult to discipline a police officer? But also, what goes through the minds of the men and women who have taken the oath? Why are officers of the state saying they have had enough? Why is the suicide rate among police officers so high that, in the profession, people talk about a suicide wave?

Using the anonymity of the internet, Valentin was able to register under his real name to apply for a post as an adjoint de sécurité (ADS; assistant security officer) the contract staff on the lowest rung of the ladder. His training at the Saint-Malo Police School lasted only three months, compared to the average of twelve months required to become a police officer. According to his instructor, the training was designed to launch a "low-cost police force" onto the streets. Proof of this, if it were needed, is the fact that training in supporting victims of domestic violence was dispensed within three hours.

When he left the school, Valentin did not get the posting he had hoped for. So he waited for a year until he could finally be posted to the commissariat of the nineteenth arrondissement of Paris; he wanted to be a cop in a working-class neighbourhood, where the police are said to have a difficult relationship with the locals.

From his very first day, the undercover reporter felt as though he had joined "a crew" aboard a rudderless ship. He was shocked. Fellow officers routinely insulted and beat people they called "the bastards", most of them Black, Arabic, or immigrant, young men. The "code of ethics of the police officer and the gendarme" he had been taught at the police-training school seemed as if it had been written for a different world, a world of bureaucratic red tape far removed from reality.

Cop depicts the day-to-day life of a police officer trapped between the devil and the deep blue sea. On the one hand, the apathy of senior officers; on the other, the hostility of a section of the population. Valentin and his fellow officers worked in a run-down commissariat, and drove ancient, battered police cars. At the end of every month, the paycheck would arrive: €1,340 euros after tax. A senate report published in 2018 noted that, at the start of their careers, police officers posted to the Île-de-France area often slept "five to a twenty-square-metre room [...] and sometimes in their vehicles".

During the time that Valentin was embedded in the commissariat, a colleague on holiday loaded his service revolver and put a bullet in his own brain. This was just one among the fifty-nine suicides in the police force in 2019 — 60 per cent more than in the previous year.

Valentin pulls no punches. He recounts simple mistakes, but also how he participated in making a false statement to cover for a fellow officer. This is at the heart of what it means to go undercover. In uncovering secrets known only to the police, the reporter opens the door to a room where no member of the public is ever admitted.

To avoid any possible retaliations, and any infringement of the private lives of his former colleagues, Valentin has changed the names of all the officers mentioned in the book. All physical features, names, and nicknames have been changed — as have all street addresses.

This book is a testimony to our times. It comes during the first term of President Emmanuel Macron, which has seen a wave of police brutality against the *gilets jaunes* (yellow vests). In fact, in 2020, twenty thousand people gathered outside the High Court in Paris to protest against police brutality, to chants of "Black Lives Matter". At the same time, investigative reports published by *Mediapart*,[1] radio Arte,[2] and *StreetPress*[3] revealed numerous examples of racist and discriminatory statements made by police officers.

Given the anger prompted by this catalogue of abuse, Macron asked the minister for the interior,

Christophe Castaner, to submit proposals designed to "improve the code of conduct of the police force". The following day, the minister in question said: "In the past weeks, too many people have failed in their duty to the republic. There have been revelations of racist insults and discrimination. This is unacceptable." For the first time, the man dubbed France's "first cop" admitted there was a problem in the ranks: a racist problem.

Infiltrating the police force? Many might think the intent of the project was hostile. You have only to read *Cop* to realise that this is not the case. Valentin reports what he sees, hears, and feels: he puts human face to the police officers as well as the victims of their abuse.

Over the days, Valentin finds that the way he speaks and acts is changing. Is this the beginning of an esprit de corps?, he wonders. A sign that his empathy has been dulled? Valentin Gendrot is surprised to find the police force infiltrating him.

GEOFFREY LE GUILCHER,

CLARA TELLIER SAVARY,

AND JOHANN ZARCA

TRANSLATOR'S NOTE

The forces of law and order in France are structured very differently from those in the United Kingdom and the United States. The French have two national police forces: the Police Nationale, a civilian police force with jurisdiction in cities and large urban areas, and the Gendarmerie, a branch of the French armed forces, responsible for both public safety and policing small towns and villages. A third service, the Police Judiciare, staffed by plain-clothes detectives, is broadly analogous to the British Criminal Investigation Department. They are an independent unit, but work with both the Police Nationale and the Gendarmerie.

The Police Nationale have jurisdiction over specific areas, each of which has a commissariat (local police headquarters). These are staffed by regular officers of varying ranks, and "security assistants", known as ADSs, who have limited powers. Within each commissariat, there are specific squads assigned to serious crimes, policing sensitive neighbourhoods, and dealing with petty crimes and fines.

The French legal system is also different. When a suspect is arrested, the judiciary work with the police, appointing a *juge d'instruction* (investigating magistrate), whose role is to question witnesses and oversee the investigation, before referring the case to a *procureur* (public prosecutor), who decides whether or not to bring charges.

1

"What the fuck did you do?"

Toto grabs the guy and slams him against the bus shelter. He's clearly about to kick the shit out of him. All around, rubberneckers stop to watch: some take out their mobile phones and film the scene.

"Get over there," François roars at me. "We need to set up a cordon."

It is one of my first days with the group, and they've finally got their hands on one. They call them "the bastards". And when the group goes out on patrol, they're going on a *bastard hunt*. Toto didn't have to break much of a sweat to catch this one. He is a skinny, puny guy, probably a minor. A *little bastard*.

I keep an eye on the perimeter. No one can be allowed to disturb them. My jaw is clenched. I keep my hands on my hips, the left hand a few inches from my gun. The scrawny kid's friends stand in front of me, glaring. I'm sweating and shaking. I feel adrenaline pumping. My heart is hammering.

"You'll have to go round," I say firmly to the

1

pedestrians walking towards me. "There's no way through."

I turn around: the guy is still pinned against the bus shelter. The incident seems interminable.

"Right, let's move," says François from behind me.

The six of us climb back into the white police van, taking the kid with us. Toto floors the accelerator. In the back, we're sent flying from our vinyl seats. You have to hang on. The terrified young man is sitting between us. There's no question of anyone else laying a finger on him; this is clearly something to be settled between Toto and the kid.

We drive at top speed along the main thoroughfares of Paris and out of our sector; I don't recognise where we are. We get to Pantin. What the fuck are we doing here? We're not supposed to leave the nineteenth arrondissement …

Toto parks in the middle of the street. He gets out, opens the sliding door, and climbs into the back of the van with us. He grabs the kid and yanks his hair.

"So, what exactly did you do back here, huh?"

One of the other officers tells me to get out and keep watch. I get out, slide the door closed, and wait. The vehicle shakes, I hear screams. I wait for a couple of minutes, keeping an eye on the comings and goings of passers-by. The door opens again, and a cop's voice bellows: "Right, maybe that'll teach you. Now, go on, get the fuck out!"

The kid gets out, he is bent double, clutching his head. He seems disoriented. He mutters: "Is that ... the French police?"

We leave him there, alone, several kilometres from where we picked him up. It's part of the punishment.

I've barely been wearing the uniform of a contract security officer for two weeks, and here I am, complicit in the beating of a young migrant. Just where is this story going to lead me? I go back and sit in the van.

"He hit me in the eyebrow with his mobile phone," Toto explains. "It happened as I was getting out at La Villette, when you guys were checking the papers of the two migrants. I mean ... I don't think he did it on purpose."

"Don't sweat it. Guys like him, they'd be better off dead," spits Bison.

Police officers are obliged to give an account of every intervention or "assignment". Using software called the Digital Activity Log, they transcribe in minute detail every event and action that takes place on shift. We call that "IM" ("incident management"). Today's incident will never be logged. First, because it is an "unexpected" incident, an initiative on the part of my fellow officers. Second, because this is what police solidarity means: what happens in the van stays in the van.

Well, not always. Not this time.

2

Monday 4 September 2017, 6.58 am.

"Who the fuck sent you, you fucking journo hack?" Behind the wheel of my filthy-white Renault Clio littered with empty takeaway cartons, I imagine how I would be lynched if I were outed professionally. I'm running late, so I step on the accelerator, heading for the National Police Academy at Saint-Malo, a hundred kilometres from my parents' house. Back to school.

I figure that if I'm found out, I'm likely to pay dearly. The long arm of the law might smash my face in. Those more furious might break my hands to stop me from writing — or, worse, put a bullet between my eyes and fake a shooting accident. When you're scared, you always imagine the worst, to the point of losing all reason.

I light a cigarette. I try to remember how I came up with the idea of going undercover in the police force. I can't think. There was the Paris demo on 1 May 2016. In the back of my throat, I can still taste the acrid tear gas tossed by the CRS — the riot police. That feeling of suffocation before I caught my breath again.

In fact, I've got my fair share of memories of protest marches. On the marches, I would watch the police officers, stiff and impassive as Robocops on standby, capable of blocking a street for half a day. I didn't envy them. As a teenager, my rather clichéd feeling was that they were defending the established order while those marching with me were fighting for change. Then I grew up. My hostility turned to curiosity.

If you'd Googled the word "police" any time over the past five years, you'd have found a series of explosive and polarising search results: soaring popularity in the wake of the Charlie Hebdo attacks, before support nosedived with the brutal treatment of the *gilets jaunes*. There are pictures of officers marching to protest their working conditions. And then there are stories of the shocking suicide rate in the police force, much higher than the average in France. Victims or executioners? Heroes or scapegoats? I became fascinated by their working conditions. So, on a Wednesday morning in March 2017, I took the plunge. I looked up the police recruitment website, lapolicenationalerecrute.fr, and registered.

I've always heard my father talk about "pigs", about "the filth" and "blue shops" — a reference to "Magasins Bleus" a brand of clothing sold by door-to-door salesmen he remembered from his childhood. His military service left him with a visceral loathing of law and order, authority, and the clack of heels on tarmac.

When I told my father about my plan, he didn't understand. How could I even think of donning an officer's cap? It had been difficult enough to get him to comprehend the dangerous lure of going undercover, the strange need to slip into another person's skin in order to tell their life story. This was worse. Picturing his son as a cop. What I was suggesting was unthinkable.

"You're crazy," he said. "The army and the police force are nothing but a refuge for alcoholics and racists."

I let him rant as I stared at the top of his head. Despite multiple sessions of chemo, and the cancer that had been eating away at him for five years, when he got worked up like this, he seemed utterly alive. But he was very frail as he sat opposite me at the cherrywood kitchen table.

"What kind of living do you think a cop makes, huh?' I said. "What exactly are the intolerable working conditions they're always complaining about? I want to find out."

I wasn't trying to persuade him; I was trying to provoke him.

I toss the cigarette out the car window. I glance at myself in the rear-view mirror. Do I pass?

I've done almost nothing to change my physical appearance before going undercover. But, out of superstition, I changed my glasses. I put aside my round steel-framed glasses for a rectangular pair with black frames. They give me a harsher, less intellectual look. Mostly, they work like a mask. I also had my hair cut very short, barely a centimetre long. I look dumb, my forehead is too high to suit a crop. I miss my light-brown curls.

I decide not to go to the dentist to have a broken premolar fixed. I'll show up at the police academy with a gap in my teeth, the legacy of a sweet tooth. If anyone finds my accent suspicious, they'll by reassured that I obviously don't have the money to visit a dentist. I try to anticipate everything; better too much than too little. They're trivial details, but I find them reassuring; they help me believe in the character I'm creating.

I would happily have driven around a little longer, but I've just reached the outskirts of Saint-Malo. I know the town well. I worked here selling second-hand goods before becoming a journalist. It's the perfect tourist location, known for its historic ramparts, its old town, its half-timbered houses, and its past as a haven for corsairs.

I pull into a free car park next to the academy. In my wheeled suitcase, I've got some T-shirts and a couple of pairs of jeans. I'm wearing a tough guy's leather jacket. Or at least that's the impression I'm hoping to give. I've left my notebooks back on my desk. For the first few days, I'll use the Notes app on my phone. I'm starting to stress out; I spark up another cigarette.

Behind thick outer walls and imposing gates, the massive freestone building rises up. Only service vehicles are allowed inside the compound. Through the grim, grey weather — a typical Breton mix of mist and mizzle — another recruit approaches the gates, his hair wet, carrying a heavy rucksack. He enters through an archway near the checkpoint. It's almost 8.00 am.

"You're cutting it fine," the officer at the desk says. "We'll let it go this time. Name?"

"Gendrot."

"Gendrooooot …" He runs a finger down the list. "Ah, here you are. ADS, class 115, section 1."

3

It feels like stepping into a barracks. Behind the high walls, there is a parade ground with the French tricolour fluttering atop a mast and, in the distance, a helipad marked by a huge white "H" painted on the ground. I pick up my kit — polo shirts, boots, belt — from some guy who works with the ISU (Internal Security Unit), then go into the four-storey building to find my dorm.

Second floor, room 205. The names of the seven occupants are marked on the door. This floor is reserved for men. Female officers are on the floor below.

I'm the last to arrive in the dorm, so I get the worst bed — the one right next to the door. There are four bunks on the left, and three on the right, separated by a line of wardrobes. Each recruit also has a small wood or metal desk. The dorm looks like something in a holiday camp. The only luxury in this rough-and-ready place is the view. From the toilets, you can see the seagulls gliding over the English Channel.

Alexis — a lanky streak of piss with a big nose — is already sprawled on the bunk next to mine, staring at his phone. He has just kicked off his shoes, and the stench is palpable. A guy called Clément, blond with dazzling white teeth, is wandering around in a pair of flowery boxer shorts. So much for atmosphere. Then there's Michel, a squat cube of pure muscle. The youngest recruit is twenty-one; the oldest, at twenty-nine, is me. "Gramps!" one of my new roommates instantly nicknames me. I smile.

4

A man with a gaunt face and an aquiline nose marches into the classroom. We all stand to attention.

"Sit," he says offhandedly.

He introduces himself: Goupil. Brigadier-Chef Goupil. He will be our instructor for the next twelve weeks, though two others will oversee sports and shooting lessons. Chef Goupil gives us a rundown of the programme for the day. First, he will lead the induction course, and then the head of the training school will give a speech. He gets right to it.

"Can anyone list the four professional situations we will deal with during your training course. Anyone?"

A young woman in the front row raises her hand.

"Dealing with the public?"

"Yes, that will be the first order of business. Carry on ..."

"Conducting a patrol, taking part in road-safety programmes, and, lastly, questioning a suspect."

"Thank you."

• • •

Recruits applying to be police officers undergo a year of training, during which they are taught to deal with seventeen professional situations. For those like us, applying to be an adjoint de sécurité (ADS; the equivalent of a Police Community Support Officer — popularly known as "rent-a-cops"), this list is slashed to four. In addition, there are fitness programmes (boxing, wrestling, running, and firearms training), and lessons in criminal law — principally the police code of ethics — all punctuated by written evaluations. We are also given hundreds of pages of photocopied lecture notes.

In less than three months, we will leave the training school, authorised to carry an automatic weapon in a public place. According to our instructor, three months is a bare minimum. He feels that this express training course will lead the way to "cut-price cops".

The post of ADS, created in 1997, allows those with no professional qualification to work in the police force. There is only one requirement: you must be under thirty.

Originally, "contract cops" were assigned desk jobs and handled the thankless bureaucracy for the force. These days, they can just as easily find themselves on the streets, like any other officer. On the beat, an ADS is allowed to stop and search, to handcuff, frisk, and question a suspect. But an ADS cannot press charges.

The rank of ADS— three-months' training and let loose on the streets — is nowhere to be found in the organisational chart of the Police Nationale. Once in uniform, the only way to distinguish an ADS from a regular officer is the blue stripe — a pale-blue rectangle the size of a métro ticket. Of the 146,000 actively serving officers in France, at least 12,000 are "contract cops".

An ADS working in Paris takes home an average of €1,340 a month; elsewhere in the country, this falls to €1,280. Like all the other recruits in my class, I have signed a three-year contract, which can only be renewed once. Should I unexpectedly discover that I have a vocation, I can apply to become a full officer, which would see me take home a monthly salary of €1,800 in the first year.

There were several reasons for my decision to apply to be an ADS. In the first place, the application process was simple: tests in reading, writing, and arithmetic; a basic physical; and interviews with three officers and a psychologist. Second, a training schedule of three months — as opposed to a year — guaranteed that I would quickly be in active service. Lastly, as an ADS I could choose to resign without having to repay my training costs.

"To keep the old dears happy, we need to send out the blues," says Chef Goupil.

To send out the blues means to flood the streets with uniformed officers, but also, figuratively, to send out raw recruits. As cops, our purpose is to stand there and look pretty, stationed outside public buildings, pedestrian precincts, and high-risk areas.

A baby-faced youth in the second row yawns.

"Ten-shun!" barks Goupil, drawing a line on the blackboard, a line for every yawn. Five ticks, and the whole section will be out doing push-ups on the freezing parade ground.

Goupil moves between the tables, handing sheets of paper to the recruits. At the top of the page is the word "Autobiography".

"I want each of you to give an account of their life so far. Nothing you say will go beyond these four walls — it's just a way of getting to know you better."

I pick up my sheet of paper and start recounting a life. Not the life where I studied for a degree in journalism at the University of Bordeaux, where I moved to Canada because I fell in love with a girl and lived there for six months, where I worry about my father's fragile health. No, I invent a life only peppered with actual events. I write about a past in which I spent six years working at a second-hand shop — in fact, I only worked there during summer holidays while I was a student. I mention the fact that the shop went bankrupt. This is also true. "Now, I want to become a police officer to defend my country against the threat of terrorism." I include a scattering of spelling mistakes, anything so I can stay under the radar.

Goupil collects the papers and, without the hint of a smile, growls: "I can size you up in twenty seconds. If I've got the slightest doubt about you, you'll get to speak for two minutes. After that, we're done."

I feel a knot in my stomach.

5

By the next morning, Alexis had given me another nickname: Snore-o-matic.

"You were puffing like a steam engine all fucking night," he mumbles, his big nose still buried in his pillow.

It's 06:25 hours. I slept like a stone, woken only briefly in the early hours by an itch from the rough blanket rubbing against my legs. I shower, shave, head down for breakfast in the self-service canteen, then go back to the dorm to put on my uniform.

My bunkmates and I fiddle with our police uniforms. We watch each other. I sense the pride they feel at putting on the uniform, the impression of belonging to a unit, a force, to something greater than themselves.

"You've got a face on you like a cop," one of my bunkmates says, flashing me a smile.

Sitting on the edge of his bed, Mickaël is threading the laces through the hooks of his boots. "Thanks," I say, reassured to know that at least I look the part, as I tuck my blue shirt into my uniform trousers. And it's true — as soon as I'm suited and booted, I feel a little like a cop.

I nip out for a quick cigarette and, at precisely 7.45, I'm out on the parade ground, standing to attention with the others, watching the raising of the flag. It's called the "ceremony of colours". The French tricolour is hoisted to the top of a white metal flagpole. It is a solemn moment. The silence is broken only by the clack of rope against steel.

"At *ease!*"

We all shift our left feet slightly to the left, our hands interlaced behind our backs. This piece of choreography will be repeated every day, before and after class.

• • •

In the force we take no fools!
In the force we take no fools!
We take some meatheads, them's the rules!
We take some meatheads, them's the rules!

We have been marching in step for ten minutes beneath the driving rain. Brigadier-Chef Bellion, our training instructor, has us march in a wide circle: the parade ground of Saint-Malo Police Academy.

Before we get up to sing at the top of our lungs, Bellion gives us a quick run-down of his CV. A former member of the BAC — the equivalent of the serious crimes squad — this hulk of a man served for more than a decade in Seine-Saint-Denis.

Standing in the middle of the parade ground, he smiles.

"Louder! *The only way we learn to march ...*"

The tallest recruits are at the back; the shortest at the front. Being about five foot ten puts me in the third row. Steel-capped boots clatter on the tarmac.

"Eyes front!" Bellion roars. "Not bad, not bad. But I reckon we can do a bit better."

At the slightest misstep, we have to start over. And over, and over.

• • •

All quiet in dorm 205. Everyone has headed down to the gym before dinner. I decided to prop myself up on my bed and watch season one of *The Sopranos* on my portable DVD player.

Romain is also in the dorm room, sitting by the window that overlooks the parade ground, rosary beads in hand, praying. Last night, I discovered that my bunkmate is a devout Catholic. I've already seen him praying twice.

On the way back to the dorm, he talks to me about his former life, when he hung out with guys who collected Third Reich memorabilia — busts of Hitler and Nazi flags. The conversation was prompted by seeing one of the recruits wearing a black sweatshirt embroidered with the letters 'SS'. It's the kind of thing

Romain has often seen before — fascist gear disguised as sportswear.

"Where I come from, it felt cool to hang out with guys who were, like, twenty when I was still at school," he explained.

He didn't always feel comfortable in the gang, and decided to cut all ties with them after they beat up a young Arab woman. "She was pregnant," he said.

"After that, I left and came up to Paris to study. The first person in the capital to talk to me was an Indian guy. A week later, he invited me to dinner with his parents. When I was leaving, his mother cried. I asked her why. She said, 'Because you're a beautiful person.'"

He tells this story in a soft voice. He has delicate features and exudes a kind of serenity, an imperturbable calm. I find him fascinating. I'm tapping on my phone, and I pull up an article in *Le Monde* about how the National Front first got a foothold in the area he comes from. He smiles.

"I was heavily involved in the junior wing of the National Front, but I chucked it in. The night of the second presidential debate, Le Pen was completely pathetic …"

Romain sighs, still frustrated by this episode. He had given so much to the party.

"One thing's for certain, I won't be voting for the NF again, even though I'll still vote right wing," he says, "The people I can't stand are communists and antifa.

They're parasites. They smoke, they drink, they don't work."

Romain hadn't gone down to the gym because he'sd been waiting for a phone call from his girlfriend. They met when he was at the training school for the Gendarmerie — in the end, he decided to transfer to the Police Nationale, and she decided to stay. He seems head-over-heels in love.

"Things between us are pretty complicated … Damn, that's her now, calling me back. 'Scuse me," he says, and leaves the dorm to take the call.

6

Five yards up ahead looms a menacing black figure. For the first time in my life, I squeeze a trigger. The gun spits out the spent cartridge and, although I'm wearing noise-cancelling headphones, I'm startled by the muffled bang. My body flinches, and the recoil pushes me back three feet as the metal casing from my 9mm clatters a few inches away. I'm boiling hot. My first bullet has lodged in the ceiling of the firing range.

The headphones block out the ambient noise. I hear the muffled voice of Cheffe Milat as though I was in a goldfish bowl. The blonde firearms instructor has to shout to make herself heard. "I'm a specialist in Brazilian jiu-jitsu," she warned us before we started the course. She will be our combat trainer.

"You need to keep your elbows locked. And you need to keep your feet firmly planted on the ground."

I concentrate, gripping the gun with both hands, my left index finger hovering near the trigger. Keeping my arms relaxed, I focus on the target, adopting the same stance as the three ADS recruits next to me.

Milat blows her whistle. We fire. My second shot clips the paper target suspended from wires. Another miss. I slide my weapon back into the plastic holster as Milat has taught us to do after each shot.

The firing range looks much like an athletics track: numbered lanes in which the white-and-tartan has been replaced by blue vinyl. We have each been issued with a Sig Sauer SP 2022. Back in 2003, Nicolas Sarkozy — then minister for the interior — decided that the national police, the gendarmes, customs and excise staff, and prison warders should all be issued with the same gun. The Swiss-German company Sig Sauer won the tender, and so their gun replaced the ancient Manurhin, which looked more like the old Colt .45s of the Wild West.

Weighing in at almost two pounds, the Sig has serious heft when tucked into my belt. I feel clumsy using it. Right now, I'm beginning to worry about just how easy it is to apply to join the force. What if someone applied to join the force in order to commit a terrorist attack? Someone on a security watchlist, an anarchist, or just some knucklehead looking to take down some cops? Would they find it as easy as I have?

France is in the middle of a state of emergency, yet here I am, the proud owner of Press Card #119895, standing in a firing range, surrounded by future cops, without even having to lie about who I am. In my shoes, an evil-minded bastard could shoot the place up.

I fire again. The third bullet hits the target — right in the belly of my paper enemy. In total, I fire twenty shots, of which only eight hit home. End of lesson.

"OK, collect your spent casings and change the targets," says Milat.

We take off our headphones, and the noisy world springs back to life. I put my gun back in a wooden locker.

"You can keep your targets," the instructor calls after us. "Right, next four!"

I crumple mine into a ball and toss it in the trash. I'm not about to let the others see my pathetic results.

Before our first class using live firearms, Milat had us working with plastic replicas, teaching us how to handle them safely: all firearms should be considered loaded at all times; always keep your index finger positioned along the frame above the trigger guard (to avoid firing accidentally); always keep the firearm pointed in a safe direction.

"Hey, look, Gramps, I scored nineteen!" said Mickaël, showing me his target. "I missed the last shot. I was gutted."

The good news is that my colleagues have settled on Gramps rather than Snore-o-matic.

"Nineteen. Fucking hell, that's good," I say.

"What about you, how did you do?"

"No idea, I didn't bother counting."

7

In the dorm, Alexis is always the first person awake. This morning, he decided to climb onto my bed. I woke with a start, opened my eyes. What the actual fuck? The arsehole is resting his balls on my forehead!

Alexis is laughing like a drain. He calls the others over and shows them the selfie he's just taken. They laugh just as hard. Discombobulated, I roar, "You're a complete shit!"

Alexis is still staring down at me and smiling.

"You want to play that game?" I growl menacingly. "OK, fine, you'll see."

He's choking with laughter, his huge white teeth bared. He grabs his towel, and leaves the dorm wearing nothing but a pair of flip-flops.

Alexis is the type of guy who dreams of being posted to the Major Incident Squad, "for the adrenaline rush". In the meantime, he downs four to six protein shakes a day: he's trying to build muscle mass. Despite the protein potions, right now he looks like a beanpole. A former dog handler, he fathered his first child at

24

seventeen, but he and his ex-girlfriend live apart these days, and he only sees his daughter — his "princess" — on alternate weekends.

This guy who will soon be enforcing the law doesn't seem to understand that what he's just done is the textbook definition of a sexual assault "on an unsuspecting victim". He thinks that these kinds of humiliations dished out by an alpha male are harmless pranks.

"For fuck's sake, guys, someone open a window — this place smells like dried-up pussy," roars Clément.

8

The true ordeal begins one Friday morning during a class taken by Chef Goupil. I've been at the academy for a month and, amid the torrent of words from our instructor, I hear a phrase that chills my blood …

"I don't know whether any of you watched *Cash Investigation* on Tuesday night …"

I blush to the tips of my ears. He's talking about a documentary I made for France 2 some months ago. My one-and-only television gig — going undercover in Lidl with a hidden camera pinned to my lapel. At the end of the piece, in an act of gross stupidity, I agreed to be interviewed on camera as Raphäel, one of my middle names. How could I possibly know that, by the time the documentary was broadcast, I'd be working undercover again?

My first reflex when Goupil mentions the programme is ridiculous: I hide under the desk, pretending to pick up a pen I've dropped … Like an ostrich, I wait for the moment to pass. I wish the ground would swallow me up.

As a journalist, I've been specialising in undercover

operations since 2014. For the first piece, I worked on the production line of a chocolate factory in Villeneuve-d'Ascq. Later, I went undercover in a call centre; worked door-to-door selling gas and electricity services; did a stint as a debt-recovery agent for Cofidis; and, most recently, on the assembly line of a Toyota factory. I collected these five investigations into a book called *Les Enchaînés*.

I got the *Cash Investigation* gig through a friend. She was working for the production company making the series. The director was looking for someone to uncover working conditions at the German discount supermarket chain. During my sixth undercover operation, I was put through hell. I saw co-workers crushed and broken before they'd turned thirty, and I took orders from a software programme that whispered into my ear.

The only possible stumbling block in the investigation was not getting hired in the first place, but putting up with this dehumanising treatment for two months.

In four years, I had never been unmasked. And now, as I pretend to search for an imaginary pen under my desk, I realise my mistake. Why did I agree to talk on camera? There was every chance that my mistake was about to fuck up my most difficult undercover investigation.

Chef Goupil is talking about a different part of the programme, a case of harassment that went viral online about three days ago. Maybe he only saw the trailer.

"You might be called to deal with a case like this," he says, before changing the subject.

"Hey, Gramps, you lost something?" says Mickaël.

I emerge from under the desk.

"My pencil," I say, tonelessly.

"On the desk …"

"Fucking hell, I'm such an idiot …"

I manage to drag myself through the morning, eagerly waiting for the afternoon, when I go back to my parents' house. In the car, I breathe a sigh of relief. I focus on what will be the high points of the weekend: teasing my dad, kicking a football around, sinking a few beers with my footy mates, and leaving the police academy behind me. And I need to sleep. When that's done, everything will seem better.

Sunday evening, I reluctantly head back to the academy. I don't feel better. Backpack in hand, I push open the door of the dorm.

"Hey, hey, piglets." I fake a casual mood. "How were your weekends?"

I shake hands: Alexis, Romain, Julien, Mickaël, Clément. I come to Basile, who is standing by the window testing his new Bluetooth headphones.

"Hey, Gramps."

His voice sometimes rises to a shrill falsetto, as though it hasn't finished breaking. I pile my clothes back into the increasingly chaotic wardrobe. Toothpaste has leaked onto the case of my portable DVD player.

Basile says: "Oh, Gramps, I caught that programme Goupil mentioned on Friday night. It's weird, but there was this guy in it who was the spitting image of you."

I feel myself tense as I try to seem uninterested. I continue putting away my clothes.

"What are you on about?"

"Take a look — that's you," he says holding up his phone.

He flashes me a smile, as though he's been building up to this, marshalling the element of surprise.

"You're really a journalist. And you're going undercover in the force."

In a split-second, all the calm I built up over the weekend is shattered. I lose my self-assurance. My voice falters, my body crumples. I muster what little strength I can.

"Hey, you're right, that guy's the spit of me. But it's not me."

"Oh, it's you all right."

I deny the evidence staring me in the face. What else can I do?

Basile posts a screen capture of me in *Cash Investigation* to our Facebook group. In an instant, the twenty-eight ADS recruits in Section 1 discover that someone who bears an uncanny resemblance to me is a journalist who has just been on television.

This is my worst nightmare. I'm scared shitless.

29

9

"Go on, tell him you're a journalist, we don't give a fuck!" one of the recruits laughs. "Admit that you're this Raphäel guy."

My black coffee sits steaming in front of my eyes, which are bloodshot from lack of sleep. According to my watch, it's already 6.45; I feel like I'm wading through molasses. I'm going to have to spend the whole day lying, trying to debunk the photographic evidence.

I spent the night tossing and turning, obsessed by a single question: how can I continue my investigation? While everyone in the dorm was fast asleep, I lay staring into the darkness.

With every passing day, I feel more paranoid. I'm terrified by anodyne events. I live in fear that one of the ADS recruits will rat me out to the instructors. If Goupil shows up to training a minute late, I'm thinking: *That's it, they know who I am, they're working out how to fuck me over ... I've been unmasked.*

Then comes the Thursday morning when the officers who check the state of our beds summon my six bunkmates, but not me. *Everyone except me*. Because they didn't make their beds properly? I imagine them being given the third degree, being interrogated about my habits, about any suspicious behaviour … And, in the end … nothing. All six are told to write a report about the state of their beds. I'm spared the punishment, not the panic attack.

Sometimes, I'm my own worst enemy, like the morning when Goupil asks the class: "Which former minister was convicted of misappropriating public funds?" I raise my hand, "Claude Guéant." Goupil nods. Behind me, I hear a classmate whisper: "Fuck, maybe he really is a journalist."

10

During the weeks of training, I strike up a friendship with Musclebound Mickaël. Micka with his washboard abs, his pumped-up pecs, his fearsome deltoids. It's like he does it to compensate for the fact he's five foot three. Still, he's seriously impressive.

At the beginning of the training course, Micka and Alexis were brought together by their mutual interest in bodybuilding and the fact that both had been dog handlers. Then, gradually, they drifted apart, and Micka and I became pretty tight.

We're the same age — twenty-nine — which makes us the oldest recruits in our section. In class, he sits behind me and we talk crap, like disruptive class clowns. We're both eager for training to be over: me, because I'm worried about being unmasked, and the paranoia is exhausting; Micka, because he's never been comfortable in an academic environment, and finds the testing and the evaluations torture. So, as the days pass, Micka become smy shadow and I his. When I go out for a cigarette, he tags along and puffs on his e-cig. We spend a couple of evenings revising together. My disciple no longer minces his words when he talks about the enemy within. He refers to Arabs as "ragheads", "*bicots*", "*crouilles*". Migrants? He'd send them home "on a charter flight".

"You know what separates man from the apes, Gramps?"

"No, what?"

"The Mediterranean!"

Micka bursts out laughing. On his phone, he shows me photos of himself before his physical transformation. He looked like a shrimp, a puny little runt.

"The ideal is for your neck to be as thick as your biceps and your thighs," he explains.

During a lesson on handcuffing a suspect — "a practice that should on no account be systematic", according to our photocopied notes, Milat hands out the "bracelets", as we call them. I try them out on my new best friend.

"Hey, not too tight, you'll break my wrist," says Micka.

As the sun beats down, next to the helipad, we try out different techniques. Handcuffing a suspect who is standing, kneeling, pressed against a wall, lying on his back. On his stomach.

"What is the specific article of law relating to handcuffing?" asks Milat.

"Article 803 of the Criminal Code," says one of the recruits, quick as a flash.

"Exactly. Good work, kids, well done," Milat congratulates us.

11

One Thursday evening, we decide to watch a movie together in the dorm. Alexis finds a service streaming *The Wave*, a film recommended by Chef Goupil some days earlier, the story of a teacher who creates a repressive, dictatorial regime within his classroom, the better to denounce autocracy.[4]

The following day, before lessons at the firing range, Micka talks to me about the film.

"You know, we're a lot like them. We wear a uniform, we're visibly a group, we use signs to recognise each other."

He mimes a salute.

"When you think about it, we're an authoritarian group, too."

• • •

As future uniformed officers, we will be invested with greater powers than the average citizen. We will have the right to stop and search them, even sanction them, and take them into custody. How are we taught the responsibility that must go hand-in-hand with such powers? How are we inculcated with an ethic relevant to such a situation? The answer is the "code of ethics". Chef Goupil gives us the gist over a period of ten hours, which is about 1 per cent of the time allotted for our fast-track training.

I reread some of the notes I took during these lessons.

"The police force is the most tightly controlled institution." Among the important points, we find "obedience" (article R. 434-5). A police officer is a link in a chain of command. Orders issued by superior officers must be obeyed. The use of force (R. 434-18) is akin to that of self-defence: "Force may be used only when necessary and must be proportionate either to the ultimate goal or to the seriousness of the threat." Impartiality (R. 434-11) refers to neutrality, the absence of bias. Discrimination or profiling should play no role in police procedures. Probity (R. 434-9) relates to the ban of corruption and influence peddling.

Our duties towards the public are: "dignity, integrity, impartiality, loyalty, exemplary conduct, and, above all, respect for every individual". These are grouped together to create the acronym DIILER. It's what they call a mnemonic, a gentle nudge: spoken aloud, the acronym sounds like dealer. I'm not likely to forget it.

•••

In our theory classes, Chef Goupil talks to us about domestic violence. A highly topical issue. In 2018, one hundred and twenty-one French women were murdered by their partners or ex-partners: an average of one femicide every three days. Three is also the number of hours devoted to the subject during our training course — a change made in 2014. Before then, ADS recruits received no specific training about domestic violence.

Goupil has no time to waste. He quickly rattles off a list of specialised police services. Notably, CRIP, the service dealing with concerns for child safety. I jot down the freephone number — 3919 — for victims of domestic abuse. Another service, known as the "phoneline for people in serious difficulty", also exists. According to an article in *Le Monde* in March 2019, calls to this line have doubled in the past year.

"You'll meet a lot of dumb bastards who beat their wives," says Goupil.

And that's it. No information as to how an ordinary officer should deal with such a situation. We have time to learn how to handcuff a suspect, or fire a gun, but no time to learn how to support a woman who is the victim of domestic abuse.

In my notepad, I copy out the cycle of violence described by Goupil. A circle that marks out the stages of abuse — honeymoon, tension, explosion, denial, reconciliation. Stages that recur until a final break-up, or death.

After an hour spent on theory, Goupil ends the session with a screening of *My King*, directed by Maïwenn. The movie depicts a toxic and terrifying relationship in which the man, played by Vincent Cassel, hits his partner. Within ten minutes, Goupil leaves the room. Alexis is asleep in his chair.

12

The first postings arrive for those who applied to work in the west of France. Megan, a bolshie young woman, is being posted to a migrant detention centre — known as a Centre de Rétention Administrative (CRA). She sulks. This is not what she had hoped for; she wanted to work in a police station, but, for the time being, her job will be to watch over migrants.

"Better to spend a year working there than five years doing sentry duty, pushing a red button to open the security gates," Goupil says, trying to sound reassuring.

Another ADS recruit discovers that she is to be a court clerk at another CRA. Her boyfriend will be tasked with transporting prisoners from the centre to the court. A lot of recruits are disappointed: during training, we all forgot that we are little more than assistant officers destined for subordinate roles.

Micka discovers he is being posted to a posh village on the Normandy coast.

"Fucking bourgeois scum …" is his only comment.

I imagine his squat, musclebound frame as he patrols

the streets surrounded by fashionably dressed poodles being walked by rich, elderly women. He pulls a face.

"Fancy a quick drink?" he says.

Micka is sick to death of the schoolboy jokes that pass for wit in the dorm. And it's true that a lot of the pranks are pretty crude. I even tried to get revenge on Alexis by completely dismantling his bed and hiding the pieces all over the third floor. For this, I woke up one morning with a Post-it note on my head, "I love cock and I give free blowjobs", a penis scrawled on my forehead in permanent marker, and gel smeared over my legs. A clear sign that it was time to stop this juvenile game of one-upmanship.

I take Micka up on his offer. After a ten-minute walk, we reach the deserted old town, its streets lined with half-timbered houses, a regular picture postcard. We go into the first bar we find.

"I did a lot of stupid stuff when I was young," Micka tells me. "I nearly went off the rails, and it was a cop who sorted me out."

"What did you do?"

He reels off the nine convictions on his criminal record. Vehicle theft, dealing weed, breaking and entering … The only thing missing from his CV is a prison sentence.

"I was a loser. I even managed to get myself expelled from a last-chance school."

After his academic failures, he became an apprentice,

working in a variety of different industries where the only constant was that things never went well with his boss. Micka is hot-headed. In his last job, as a security guard, he got into too many fights with the drunks coming out of the club.

"To get into the academy, I had to appear before a commission," he says. "I played it straight, told them everything."

His colourful past means that he cannot afford to make the slightest misstep, or he will be thrown out. But the pressure has started to weigh on him. He is desperate for the training course to be over. As am I. We spend some evenings revising together. The national theory test is looming, and he is terrified.

It seems like pretty much anyone can become a cop: a journalist, an ex-fascist, and, most improbably, a guy with a criminal record. At the same time, we are not "public servants"; we are "contract cops", also known as "the gig workers of the public service". What was originally intended to be a temporary stopgap has become a permanent role; according to the Institute of National Statistics, ADSs acount for approximately one million of the 5.6 million people working in the public service.

Worst of all, despite the broad selection criteria, I nearly flunked the admission. As with Micka, my application was referred to a commission because I have limited sight in my right eye. Having studied the file, it was decided that my visual acuity of 20/200 was no impediment to my being admitted to the academy. I'm lucky that they're prepared to accept just about anyone.

•••

In the dorm, Basile is the one who has been most dogged about the whole *Cash Investigation*/undercover journalist thing. I'm doing my best to get on with him: I take him drinking, prime him with anecdotes from my (fictitious) past. But he's like a dog with a bone. I feel as though I'm permanently strapped to an ejector seat. I'm constantly on my guard, worried that I'll slip up. Sometimes, I'm afraid I'll talk in my sleep. It's exhausting.

"Hey, you know Gramps here is making a documentary," Basile jokes one night while we're all sitting around chatting in the dorm.

"Oh, fuck off and give it a rest."

Irritably, I fish out the key to the padlock on my locker.

"Here," I say, throwing it to him. "You want to go check for a camera? Go on, look. There's fuck-all in there."

I glare at him furiously. He doesn't dare respond.

"The guy on the TV wasn't me, got it? Now, if I wanted to find someone with the same dumb face as you, I don't think I'd have a problem."

He gives me a wide berth for the rest of the course.

13

The passing-out ceremony takes place on 24 November 2017. After a speech from the Préfet de Police (Chief of Police), we all toss our caps into the air. Micka introduces me to his girlfriend and his parents. In one of my endless attempts to needle my father, I had invited him to the parade. "Don't even think about it, arsehole," was his reply.

I've come twenty-seventh in a class of fifty-four — bang in the middle, safely in the soft belly of the beast. Our rankings will have no effect whatsoever on our careers in the force.

It's official: I'm a cop. On my chest and on my epaulettes, I wear the cobalt-blue stripe of an ADS, anonymous amid the mass of uniforms. By now, I know the police ranks by heart. Just above my pitiful rank as ADS comes the ordinary police officer, then Sous-Brigadier, Brigadier, Brigadier-Chef, Major, Captain, and then Commandant. At the apex of this pyramid sits the Commissaire.

I am still waiting to hear where I will be posted,

oblivious of the lands where the winds of police bureaucracy will carry me.

Four days later, the ADS recruits who asked for a posting in Paris and the Île-de-France are gathered in a lecture hall in the Préfecture de Police. We are finally going to find out our fates.

"Over the past twenty years, some 4,500 ADS officers have worked in Paris, of whom 44 per cent later successfully applied to become regular officers."

I listen to Major Castro anxiously as I wait to find out where I've been posted. Like game-show hosts, they drag out the suspense.

"When you show up to the station where you're working, bring a padlock," says an officer standing next to the major. "Because there are no thieves in the police force; only victims …"

Finally, the major begins to read the list of postings in alphabetical order. I feel my body tense.

"Gendrot?"

"Yes, sir!"

"You've been posted to the Psychiatric Infirmary of the Préfecture de Police in Paris. No one is coming to collect you; you'll have to make your own way there."

The psychiatric what-the–actual-fuck? What is this shit? It's a serious setback. My dreams of going undercover in a police station have gone up in smoke.

14

Lunatic driver. That's what I am, a driver for lunatics. A quick Google search tells me that the Psychiatric Infirmary of the Préfecture de Police in Paris (known as I3P to the initiates) is in the fourteenth arrondissement, a stone's throw from the Hôpital Sainte-Anne and La Santé Prison.

On the second floor of a building on the rue Cabanis, I take the secure-access lift and find myself in a long corridor with peeling walls. Doctors and nurses are bustling about. On their white coats, each wears the blue-and-red badge of the Paris police. They are talking about a patient who was admitted the night before.

I have a meeting with a phlegmatic woman, a health executive with the I3P. She offers a firm handshake and does not smile. I follow her to her office.

"Your main responsibility will be to transport patients to specialist psychiatric units. You will also be responsible for ensuring that the tank is filled and that the vehicle is clean."

The vehicle in question, a Citroën C8 ambulance, is parked outside.

Inside the huge police-issue rucksack I have been trailing around since I got here are my uniform, and my boots, immaculately polished and ready for action. In my left hand, I am carrying my black bulletproof vest.

"You're not going to need those," the executive explains. "Here, you'll be working in civilian clothes."

"What about my service weapon? I'm supposed to be picking it up on Friday."

"You won't need that either. There are no guns allowed here."

The executive flashes me a smile for my naïve question. She describes the flexi-time schedule: three days on, three days off.

"Your shift is from 10.00 am to 8.00 pm. If you've finished by 6.00 pm, you can request a permission slip to leave. You'll work as a team with another ADS. The I3P is a highly secure unit, so I must insist that you respect patient confidentiality, especially when there are well-known people in the facility."

The Russian agitator Petr Pavlensky ended up here in late 2017 after setting fire to the Bank of France (though some years before he claimed responsibility for publishing the sex tapes that would force Benjamin Griveaux to give up his candidacy for mayor of Paris).

I suddenly wonder what I am doing here, so far from my initial objective. Can I just wait it out for two or three months and then ask to be reassigned to a commissariat? In the context of the nine-month undercover operation I'd planned (three months at the training academy and six months working at a commissariat), this would be an acceptable extension. After all, when you go undercover, there are many unknown unknowns. As though she can read my mind, the health executive says: "ADS posting here lasts for one year."

A year! I am devastated by this new piece of information. A year is much too long. A year is out of the question. What do I do? Resign? But then, what do I do with the three months I spent at the police academy? Try to sell an article about police training? This day has gone to shit.

After our meeting, the executive invites me to come to the break room so she can explain the infrastructure. I push open a set of double doors onto a corridor lined with rooms in which the mentally ill sleep, a line of crimson doors lit by a faint glow. A cleaning lady moves from room to room, collecting meal trays.

On the left of the corridor, the kitchen; on the right, the break room. As I step inside, I see a bearded man in a blue coat.

"Hello," he smiles at me, "are you the new doctor?"

"No, I'm the new ADS …"

"Oh, you're the new driver! Welcome! My name's Jocelyn. I'm a guard."

The orderlies wear blue coats; the nurses wear

white. The guy seems nice enough, but I'm not feeling particularly social. I just want to be left alone to think.

"The best thing about this place is it gives you time to study for the entrance exams to the real police."

"True enough," I say.

My new friend does not exactly seem snowed under. He casually drifts off towards the kitchen to make himself a cup of tea. Another guy comes up to me, wearing civvies: this is Jérémy, the other ADS. Seeing my miserable expression, he smiles.

"Hey, look, I pulled exactly the same face when I first showed up here."

He briefs me about the job.

"In general, no one busts your balls here. To be able to drive the patients, you need to install an app called Waze on your phone. I'll send you a list of the hospitals we visit. They're all over the Île-de-France."

"You been here long?"

"Just over eighteen months. I've got a kid, so it's practical."

Out in the corridor, a young man in a black tracksuit is pacing in slow motion. He looks like the blond kid in Gus Van Sant's film *Elephant*. Half-hidden by a curtain of bleached-blond hair, he has a thousand-yard stare, and his tracksuit bottoms are loose and baggy. In fact, they start to slip, revealing a pair of blue Lycra boxers. His arms are strapped to his sides by a white leather belt.

• • •

A little basic research tells me that the I3P has a reputation for being a black-ops site.

"An increasingly controversial top-secret facility that allows no scrutiny from outsiders or journalists, [the I3P] is where those who present with psychiatric problems when questioned by police are 'detained'", according to Cécile Prieur in *Le Monde* in 2006.

Among the two thousand patients admitted to the Infirmary each year, most have been questioned by the police for misdemeanours. The I3P is, effectively, an emergency psychiatric unit for the Paris police. The facility, which has no counterpart anywhere in Europe, can trace its history back to the Napoleonic period, and evokes memories of *lettres de cachet* — those orders bearing the royal seal by which the king could have an undesirable person imprisoned, exiled, or incarcerated. Critics of the facility talk about arbitrary internments.

Speaking of the I3P, Claude Finkelstein, the president of the National Federation of Current and Former Psychiatric Patients, said: "It is high time to put an end to this exceptional system, which smacks of a time of royal edicts." Serge Blisko, a former member of parliament and mayor of the thirteenth arrondissement, described it as a "psychiatric policing system".

In France, someone found wandering the streets, delirious, is taken to a doctor and, if it is deemed necessary, admitted to a psychiatric facility. Except in Paris. There, the person is assessed by a UMJ (Medico-Judicial unit) before being held for an average of 24–48 hours in my new workplace.

The great Albert Londres, one of the inventors of undercover operations and investigative journalism, took a keen interest in the establishment. In 1925, he published *Among the Madmen*. Early in the book, he describes how he attempted to pass as a mentally ill patient to gain access to the Prison Special Infirmary, as the I3P was then known. He was recognised by the head doctor, and had to abandon his undercover mission.

As a result, it is highly likely that, by sheer coincidence, I am the first journalist ever to walk the halls of this unit.

Behind a door that has been bolted from the outside, a man is screaming; he is refusing to take his antipsychotic medication.

"If I take this shit, I can't get it up! I want a fucking wank. It's been twenty-one years since I last had a hard-on!"

I have to confess that this new planet peopled by strange beings has piqued my curiosity. Every time I go undercover, I like to dive into a parallel universe, an unfamiliar world. But in this case, I signed up to write about the French police.

I try to analyse the situation. My previous undercover operations never lasted more than two or three months, and, as a result, I've spent the past four years taking short-term contracts in backbreaking jobs. If I decide to stay at the Infirmary for a year, at least I will be geographically and financially settled.

Besides, my father is about to start another round of chemotherapy. If I have a stable job, at least I can spend more time with him. My work at the Infirmary is three days on, three days off, which means I could go home more often.

So I won't give up my attempt to go undercover in a police station. I've made my decision. I'll stick it out.

15

"It's a rogue's gallery, this place," a nurse called Olivier says about a patient who has just been admitted. She is in the first room on the left of the hall. From behind the door, she peers through the window of reinforced glass, watching the comings and goings. I can see her from where I'm sitting in the break room. I'm drinking my third coffee of the morning, Suddenly, she starts pounding on the door.

"Fucking Nazis! I don't belong in here, I need to get to work!"

On the first couple of occasions, a nurse or a doctor would go over and try to calm her. Not anymore.

"You, the lazy-arsed bastard in the glasses, sitting around drinking coffee."

Is she talking to me? I pretend not to notice. Next to me, Jérémy is cracking up laughing. Now she's speaking German. I recognise the language, though I don't understand a word. No one takes any notice, so she goes back to speaking French.

"I was promised something to eat!"

Someone brings her food, which she decides is "disgusting". She tosses her blankets on the ground, along with her beetroot salad. The floor is spattered with diced beetroot, and the viscous red juice trickles out into the hallway.

"We're not here to talk to the patients," a nurse tells me. "They're suffering a psychotic episode. We restrain them and we medicate them. The talking therapy comes later, at the hospital."

"At least it livens things up!" Jérémy flashes me a smile.

Eventually, a nurse comes and sedates the patient. Jérémy and I never intervene when we see such things. Our job is to drive — nothing more.

Within three weeks of my arrival, Jérémy had told me everything about his life to date. As an apprentice for ArcelorMittal at a steel-manufacturing plant, he earned €1,800 a month. But he had always wanted to be a cop. Becoming an ADS means he now takes home only €1,350. Aside from the cops who come to drop off or collect a patient, Jérémy is the only officer I see on a daily basis.

• • •

This morning, we're supposed to transfer a woman to the Hôpital Bichat in northern Paris, near the Porte Sainte-Ouen. The woman refuses to leave her room, and refuses to get dressed. She screams. A little group gathers in the hallway.

"I don't wanna go! I wanna stay here!"

Two orderlies drag her out of the room. She emerges feet first, and hunkers down in the hallway. A perfect helmet of dark hair frames her impassive face. Her blue pyjamas trail on the ground; she does not want to get into the lift.

"If you don't come quietly, you'll wind up on the floor," says one of the orderlies.

Bernard grabs the pyjama collar and sends her sprawling on the ground. None of those present say a word. She lies there, tears streaming down her face, her hair plastered over her eyes and mouth. Her pyjama top gapes to reveal her right shoulder.

Nurses rush to fetch a wheelchair. The woman is still struggling, so she has to be forced into the chair.

Downstairs, flanked by a nurse and an orderly, she climbs into the ambulance, then falls asleep. It's Jérémy's turn to drive. To kill time, I decide to ride along.

"These people, they're worse than useless. Can you imagine? There's doctors and nurses and all sorts paid to look after them, and what do they do? Nothing. They're benefit scroungers."

"They're ill," I say, coolly. "What do you suggest we do with them?"

"Bullet."

Many of the orderlies and the nurses share his

opinion. They differ only as to the method: for my colleague here, a bullet; for the others, a painless injection.

The woman does not wake until we get to the hospital fifty minutes later. She starts caterwauling again. Her vacant eyes study the hospital nurse.

"Slut, I don't like you either!"

She glances at the elderly porter.

"And you, hey you, dickhead. Don't you fucking touch me."

It takes every ounce of tact and diplomacy the nurse can muster to persuade her to sit in the wheelchair.

On the drive back, the male nurse and the orderly fall asleep in the empty ambulance. Jérémy wakes up. He talks to me about Aisne, the region he's from. According to a recent documentary on TF1, the area has been blighted by drugs.

"I knew guys at my school, guys who were good friends, who got into smack and shit like that."

He lowers his voice a little.

"I actually tried heroin myself once. But, y'know, it was a one-off thing. When I was into sport, I had a good friend, a cop, as it goes, and he used to say to me that a lot of cops are delinquents who took the right turning."

By the time we get back to I3P, it is 8.15 pm. Jérémy clocks off early. I hang around to deal with the last two patient transfers. It's an arrangement we worked out.

He tells me he's just put in for a transfer. Soon, he'll be working in another police unit, and a new ADS will be sent to replace him.

I randomly jot down the reasons for patients being admitted. Behavioural problems at home, breach of the peace, creating a disturbance at Charles de Gaulle airport. Aggravated assault on a high-speed train. Threatening a pregnant woman. Stealing a van.

I close my notebook. In this strange new world, I have to struggle to keep my journalistic reflexes in check. I am fascinated by this new reality.

Tomorrow, I have to get up early and drive back to my parents' house. My father has taken a turn for the worse these past few weeks. Now, he needs a machine to help him breathe when he moves around. The slightest effort has become agony. There will be no new round of chemotherapy; he is too weak. His face is gaunt, his spirit is flagging. At home, we have made our peace with what is to come.

16

Papá passed away one Sunday morning in March. In his hospital room, I held his hands for the last time. Those big, beautiful, burning hands that warmed me as a child, while my hands were always numb with cold. "God almighty, you've nothing in those veins of yours," he used to say. And I would go and snuggle next to him, and he would hug me gently.

I took two weeks' compassionate leave. I wavered; I needed time to myself, far from the I3P, where I felt that I was vegetating. I informed the health executive. I said nothing to my colleagues. It felt too private. I needed to keep it to myself.

17

My return to my real-fake job is gruelling. My heart is not in it; it's still weighed down by grief. I try to convince myself that this day-to-day monotony is the best possible way to get through the pain.

I twiddle my thumbs while I sit around waiting to be posted to another police department. Time stretches out endlessly. At times, I relieve my boredom by jotting down the delusional rants and conspiracy theories of the patients.

A man addled by his medications screams: "You're not men. You're fucking whores. I know you gave me AIDS with the shit you've been pumping into me!" On a different day, it is the childlike smile of an obese man that chills my blood, especially when I hear him say: "When I was little, I used to scratch my sister." He still scratches; today it was his mother. Or the homeless boy who claims to be a student at the Paris Institute of Political Studies, and whispers to me: "I wasn't feeling well, so I went to see my doctor. He told me he couldn't see me, so I punched him."

•••

There are countless people locked away inside themselves. A Turkish man ripped out one of his teeth, convinced that his wife had fitted it with a microphone so she could spy on him; a man suffering from schizophrenia was arrested at the Gare Saint-Lazare, brandishing a knife, roaring in an English accent that he had the right to cut himself "a slice of brownie".

Two of the patients stood out. First, Odile, who is a frequent flyer here. Every time she is admitted, a nurse says, "Hello, Odile, long time, no see!" Odile is fifty-eight, but looks ten years older. Her diagnosis has not changed since the first time she was admitted in 1986 — the first of fifty-one admissions. The doctors say she is suffering from "Deficit Disorder Psychosis". The more pragmatic nurses say that she suffers from "mental retardation".

Sometimes she is hospitalised, sometimes not. Homeless since the age of fourteen, she spends her life on the streets or in psychiatric units. In the space of five months, she was referred to five different facilities, mostly in Auxerre, Toulouse, and Paris. This time, she was trying to steal a wallet from a locker when she was arrested by the police.

"It's pointless keeping her in hospital; it's like pouring water into a sieve," a nurse whispers.

Then there's Bongo, who was arrested one night

for chasing people down the street with a club. A week after being released from jail, he smoked crack. When I first see him, I'm struck by how much he looks like Thierry Paulin, a serial killer who murdered old ladies back in the 1980s. Bongo has the same bleached-blond hair, the same gap between his teeth.

The I3P psychiatrist insists that he be turned back over to the police. When Bongo hears this, he freaks out and starts banging his head wildly against the door of his room.

"You're traitors, the lot of you!"

When one of the doctors comes to take his temperature, Bongo roars even louder.

"You! You're a traitor! I told you my life story!"

The doctor engages him in conversation, deliberately speaking in a low voice. I stand in the doorway and watch the scene play out. In the room, there are four orderlies. They decide that he needs to be restrained.

"He's not mentally ill," says the doctor. "He just knows that he'll be sent to the Immigration Detention Centre. That's why he's angry."

An Immigration Detention Centre is little more than a holding cell where you wait to be sent back to where you came from. For a migrant, it is the end of their dreams. Some minutes later, three cops arrive to take him away.

Those admitted to the I3P do not have the rights of a medical patient, nor do they have the full rights of a suspect in police custody. Although, in theory, they have had the right to see a lawyer since 2009, in practice, not a single lawyer comes through the doors in my fifteen months working in the unit.

When someone is admitted, they are seen by a duty doctor before being systematically sedated and physically restrained, except in those rare cases where the patient has come of their own volition. There are two forms of sedation: if the patient is calm, they are given liquid to swallow; if they struggle, the sedative is injected into the buttocks. If the patient is particularly "distraught" (code for "crazy"), a heavier dose is administered.

Once this is done, the patient is physically restrained. Between 15–17 July 2009, the I3P was subject to an inspection by the Office of the Controller-General of Prisons. The published report states: "In many cases, no explicit reason for the use of physical restraints restraint is listed in the patient's notes. Such reasons should, in all cases, be clear and unambiguous." This is an understatement, since, from what I witnessed, patients are almost systematically restrained, regardless of the reason for their admission.

The controller-general's report also noted, among other things, the lack of shower facilities for the patients, the absence of buzzers in the rooms (patients have to hammer in the door to summon a nurse), the lack of pyjamas in various sizes, and the absence of working shutters in patients' rooms …

In 2019, a new report was submitted by the controller-general. Once again, it bemoaned the "confusion" of the I3P's status as a psychiatric unit under the direct authority of the police.

The patients I saw being admitted were all misfits, many of them living on the margins of society. "They've been forgotten by God and man," as a nurse once told me. They were individuals in crisis, junkies, homeless people, immigrants, most of them destitute, predominantly from poor, working-class areas of Paris.

I spent my days off at the François-Mitterrand National Library, looking through archives about the Infirmary. A thesis written about the I3P in 1977 claims that the patients admitted are "predominantly male, young, socially and economically disadvantaged, invariably in a state of intoxication or suffering acute psychotic decompensation, who have been arrested for causing a breach of the peace." It further states: "Of these, one-third are homeless and one-third are migrant workers. In short, patients are preferentially selected from an underclass of the unemployed, the homeless, and the displaced."

Forty years on, nothing has changed.

In the long months spent waiting for another posting, I wind up forgetting that — officially — I'm a cop. Being a driver has become just another job that pays the rent. During this nebulous period, I break up with my girlfriend, move out of my shared apartment, and move to Vincennes, to a tiny studio flat measuring barely 150 square feet. As though preparing for my new life.

On the desk in my new studio, I place a photo of my father, smiling, about to crack a joke. Some days, I talk to him; it helps.

Finally, the morning comes when I can apply for a transfer. I write a few short lines stating that I wish to complete my training so that I can apply to be a fully fledged police officer: "My aim is to gain experience within a team, at a commissariat and as part of an emergency response unit, to improve my knowledge of the practical techniques and procedures of dealing with suspects."

I include a wish-list of the areas in which I would like to work in order of preference: the nineteenth, eighteenth, and twentieth arrondissements of Paris, which are reputed to be the most sensitive areas for police work.

Why the nineteenth arrondissement? In March 2016, the commissariat in that arrondissement was shaken by allegations of police brutality — a news story that caught my attention. The incident occurred during protests against controversial reforms to French labour laws, outside the Lycée Henri-Bergson, near the Parc des Buttes-Chaumont.

A viral video showed a policeman punching a secondary-school pupil in the face. The blow was so severe that that the fifteen-year-old boy fell to the ground, suffered a broken nose, and was hospitalised for six days. The footage sparked a furore, and was denounced by the minister of the interior, Bernard Cazeneuve, as "shocking". The officer involved in the altercation was given an eight-month suspended sentence, but the president of the court decided not to record the sentence on the officer's criminal record. This allowed him to continue serving as a police officer.

On the same day, another officer working in the same commissariat, having been pelted with flour and eggs, "kicked the legs out from under" a young man, then grabbed another by the throat and dragged him thirty yards. On 24 May 2018, two years after the incident, the officer was given a four-month suspended sentence and was forced to pay damages to his victims amounting to €600 and €700 respectively. He, too, was allowed to continue serving as a police officer.

One detail about the case particularly struck me: all of the accused officers' colleagues testified that they had not witnessed any violent acts. The prosecutor who argued for the officer to be given a suspended sentence referred to this solidarity between officers as a "code of silence".[5]

I was granted the first choice on my wish list.

18

I have to suck in my belly to button up the navy-blue uniform trousers. Fifteen months of enforced idleness at the I3P has added several kilos to the toned, fit body I had when I left the police academy. The trousers feel tight across my hips. It is 1.40 pm, Saturday 9 March 2019. In twenty minutes, I will start my first shift as an officer at the commissariat in the nineteenth arrondissement.

I had been summoned to the police station three days earlier. There were three ADS officers competing for a single job working on the beat. The other two roles involved pushing paper for the four hundred officers at the station, or manning the reception desk of a unit whose name I can't remember. Two jobs that involved no active police work. If I'd been given one of these non-jobs, I would have handed in my resignation.

As it turned out, I was lucky. Thanks to my length of service, I was allowed to choose my posting. I chose to work on the streets. My two colleagues were clearly disappointed. Shortly after this latest panic, we met with the Commissaire Divisionnaire (a rank equivalent to Chief Superintendent) who gave us a brief summary of the workings of the station. "The nineteenth arrondissement, with a population of 190,000, is the second-largest administrative area of Paris," she recited tonelessly, her thick-rimmed glasses perched on her nose. "The primary problems we face in this district involve delinquency, drugs, and prostitution. These are dealt with by the four hundred officers working in this commissariat."

I pull on my light-blue polo shirt. On the left sleeve, I pin the red, white, and blue badge of the Police Nationale. On the right sleeve, I pin one that reads "City of Paris Public Security" and a motto "Aid, Serve, Protect". The back of the shirt is emblazoned with the word "POLICE" in large black letters.

In the basement changing rooms, I have been assigned locker number 488. This is where I keep my black rucksack and my civilian clothes. All around me, other cops are getting changed. Some are finishing their shifts; others are just starting. No one says a word. One of the officers is glued to his phone. I buckle my belt.

I go upstairs, through two sets of double doors, and step into "the incident room", the hub of the commissariat, which is off-limits to the public. A large, open-plan space, it serves as an office.

The place is ramshackle and old-fashioned: pale-wood panelling, a white floor encrusted with layers of grime. There are two men handcuffed to a black bench. There are fifteen officers, including the three seated behind a long counter. I do not know a single person. The only thing that signals that I belong here is my uniform.

I am surprised by the appearance of the other officers. Most of them look younger than me. Three are sporting carefully trimmed beards. Most have short hair, graduated at the temples and around the ears. With my clean-shaven face, my glasses, and my scrawny arms, I look out of place. While I might have passed muster at the police academy, here I look like a schoolboy.

The officers stare at me in silence. I adopt the guarded expression of a contract cop among hardcore police officers.

"I need to pick up my service weapon," I say to one of the officers sitting behind the counter. "What do I need to do?"

"Get the keys to the gun case where your gat is kept," comes the curt response.

Behind two heavy white doors, I track down my gun case among the dozens of others. Inside is my Sig Sauer and two clips.

I go into a small soundproofed room to service the pistol. It had been so long since I've had to do this that I'd forgotten the safety rules, so I watched a YouTube tutorial the night before. I focus on my task: I don't want to look like a complete numpty.

To check there is no bullet lodged in the barrel, I fire the gun into the sandbox provided for this purpose, slide back the breech with a "clack-clack", load one of the clips, and chamber a round so the gun is ready for use. I slip the two pounds' weight into my belt, and slide the second clip into my right pocket.

"Hey, big guy, don't forget to sign for," calls the cop who gave me the keys to the locker. "What's your number?"

"299 145."

He types the number into his computer.

"All good, you can sign."

"What's it for?"

"It's to confirm that you checked out your weapon. You'll need to check it back in tonight, at the end of your shift."

I start out on "sentry duty": me and another cop are posted behind metal barriers outside the station; our duty is to check visitors' bags and ask them why they are visiting. Outside, I run into my colleague. His name is Radha. He has piercing eyes and a wiry, muscular physique, and his hair is almost completely shaved.

"When did you get here?" he asks, nervously puffing on his cigarette.

"Today's my first day."

He does not rise. From the single diagonal stripe on his chest, I know that he's a trainee officer. After one year's service, he will be given a permanent posting.

On the rue Erik-Satie, pedestrians come and go, and kids play in a nearby schoolyard. It is quiet. I am wearing a special bulletproof vest, "a heavy-duty vest," lined with ceramic plates capable of stopping a bullet from an assault rifle. Wearing it makes me feel vulnerable. I realise that I'm a potential target. In recent years, there have been several incidents in which terrorists have targeted cops — in 2016, two officers were killed in Magnanville.[6]

An elderly woman walks up to us and dispels this thought: "Good morning, officers. Last Thursday, my husband said, 'I'm going to kill you.' He's not a well man, and he's often in a bad mood, but still, I thought I should file a report."

Radha tells her that it is too late to report the incident. "There's nothing the police can do."

I try to find out a little more.

"Has he ever hit you? Because if he has …"

"Come back and see us if it happens again," Radha cuts me off.

The woman leaves without filing a complaint.

Having taken the three-hour module on domestic violence, I'm all too aware of how little training officers are given on the subject. Radha has just sent away a woman whose husband threatened to kill her. I spend my first hour on duty trying to stay calm.

On 13 February 2020, the Ministry of the Interior published a report titled "Support for victims of domestic abuse in police stations and gendarmeries". The figures look like the election results from a tin-pot dictatorship: according to the report, 90 per cent of victims considered the support offered in police stations and gendarmeries "satisfactory", 90 per cent claimed that they had no difficulty in filing a complaint, while 76 per cent of victims considered the time accorded them was satisfactory.

The report elicited a strong reaction from Albane Gaillot, the member of parliament for Val-de-Marne — who can hardly be accused of bias, since she is a member of the governing party, La République en Marche. On 18 February 2020, Gaillot wrote to the minister of the interior, Christophe Castaner:

> Reactions from organisations that offer support to victims of domestic abuse have been unanimous: these figures — as pleasing as they might sound — bear no relation to the reality they observe on a daily basis. The appeal for witness statements by Le Groupe F[7] in March 2019, which elicited more than 500 responses from almost every département in France, paints a very different picture, with some 91 per cent of cases being handled poorly. Officers refusing to file complaints, making light

of violence, etc. … I cannot help but wonder about the criteria underpinning this report when all those consulted during our conference on domestic violence stated that urgent work was needed in dealing with victim support in police stations and gendarmeries.

"You've only just got here," my colleague pulls me up short. "Right now, you need to watch and see how things work. You're here to observe."

Other members of the public follow: a man wants to report the theft of his phone; Radha checks his briefcase and lets him in. A woman comes to report that teenagers have been racing their mopeds outside her house; she complains that the police have done nothing. A man shows up looking for his mother, who suffers from Alzheimer's, who has been missing for two hours. A lawyer comes to consult with a client in custody.

Between inquiries, Radha and I barely speak. He asks where I was posted before this, and I tell him about the psychiatric facility. He doesn't seem interested. My bulletproof vest weighs on me like lead.

Our first hour of sentry duty ends at 3.00 pm, and two other officers take our places. We will be back on duty in an hour, and will alternate for the rest of the day. One hour on duty, one hour off.

I watch as Radha wanders towards the garage to smoke a cigarette.

"We'll need to do inventory later," he says.

"What's that?"

"I'll explain later."

Back in the commissariat, I take my position behind the counter. I discover we don't use the word "counter"; we say "the bench". Behind me, a door opens onto a hallway lined with cells for those in custody, those drying out, and those being searched. The names of those in custody are scrawled in blue letters on a whiteboard. They are held in five different cells. Opposite the bench is a series of doors that lead to rooms equipped with computers where statements are taken, and to storage areas for equipment and weapons. The last double door leads to the reception area, where members of the public can come to file a complaint, request a power of attorney, or raise any other business. Senior officers are on the upper floors.

I quickly realise that sitting behind the bench mainly involves clock-watching. Next to me, an officer with a crew cut and a greying beard is silently playing on his phone.

"Hey, Bullitt!" shouts a passing officer.

Bullitt? Like the Steve McQueen movie? Weird nickname.

"What? What's happening?" he roars back.

"Are you the duty officer?"

The duty officer, as Radha explained earlier, is the person who assumes responsibility in the event of a problem — if there's trouble with a prisoner in custody, for example, or if something recovered during a search later disappears. The duty officer also registers prisoners on probation who report to the station.

"Yeah, yeah, course I am. Who were you expecting? Everyone else round here is a loser."

Bullitt bursts out laughing. He is nervous and edgy, as though mounted on springs. The three white stripes on his uniform mark him out as a Sous-Brigadier — equivalent to Deputy Sergeant, the highest rank for an ordinary officer. "Ball-bags", we were taught to call them at the academy.

One of the prisoners starts pounding on the door of his cell, and Bullitt gets annoyed.

"Can someone shut that fucker up? They get on my tits, swear to god!"

The prisoner carries on hammering on the reinforced glass. Bullitt gets to his feet, and strides down the hallway that stinks of piss and damp. I follow. He unlocks the cell door, grabs the prisoner by the hair, and drags him into the custody suite.

"Shut the fuck up!" he roars.

Bullitt gives him a slap across the face, and then another, harder slap. I feel a knot in my stomach. I watch without saying a word. Then Bullitt drags the man back to his cell. Order is restored. Ball-bags sits down in his chair. None of the other officers so much as flinches. Is beating a prisoner a routine occurrence?

As a rookie cop, I'm stunned by what has just happened. In my world, what I've seen is a rare flash of violence. Here, no one even troubles to look up.

Back on sentry duty outside the station, Radha and I are approached by a woman from the Red Cross accompanied by a foreign minor.

"He's fifteen, and he's from Guinea," she says. "Can you find him a bed in a hostel?"

"It's a bit early," says Radha. "You'll have to wait until early evening to see if there are any beds free."

The woman and the boy go into the station, settle themselves on metal chairs, and wait. I ask Radha to explain what he meant earlier by "inventory".

"Inventory is when we tally up all the stolen cars, bikes, or mopeds we've seized that no one collected. When you're on sentry duty, you have to do an inventory once a day when you're stationed behind the bench. Oh, and we're the ones who have to take the rubbish out at the end of the shift."

Inventory, Radha explains, is one of a number of "chores" — the things to be done when not out on the beat. As an ADS, I'll have to do a lot more chores than fully fledged officers — and therefore spend less time on the streets.

• • •

Ten o'clock. The end of my first day. The kid looking for

a bed in a hostel is still sitting on the metal chair. The woman from the Red Cross has left.

"Shit, I completely forgot about him," says Bullitt, who is filling in a report about a stolen Mercedes.

I sign the register to certify I've checked in my service weapon, then store it in the gun case. In the changing room, I strip off my uniform. I've spent the day watching, trying to make sense of how the station functions, trying to memorise names by associating each officer with some detail of their personality: Bullitt-the-hothead, Radha-the-resentful …

And then there are the countless acronyms that pepper every other sentence "VPN", "AVP", "CJ", "STP", like a foreign language. I'll need to write up a glossary if I'm to find my way around. I've barely done anything, yet I feel completely shattered. What will it be like when I'm out on patrol?

19

Atten-TION! Chin up, chest out, shoulders back, stomach in, arms fixed by my sides, feet together, I stand motionless. It's 6.30 am. Two Brigadiers-Chefs — the equivalent of Sergeants — step into the incident room. They call out the orders and the teams for the day. This dawn ritual lasts five minutes. When an officer is addressed by name, he must say "received". The rank and file stand in three rows.

This Tuesday — my fourth day at the commissariat — will be my first out on patrol.

During roll-call, I'm told I'll be part of Alpha Patrol. I'll be driving around in a police van with five other officers: Sylvain (aka Bison, our Captain), Loïc, Toto, a guy with a northern accent nicknamed Tacos, and a female officer I haven't seen before. Of the thirty or so officers in my brigade — the J3 — there are rarely more than twenty on active duty at any one time. And of those twenty, only a handful came over and introduced themselves to me. So, right now, most of my fellow officers are still complete strangers. As are all the officers in J2 and J1, the other two daytime brigades, not to mention the night brigade.

The two Brigadiers-Chefs who assign duties ensure that I am settling in, and regularly ask how things are going.

We pile traffic cones, reinforced bulletproof vests, and two riot shields into the back of the vehicle, then set off through the streets of Paris. In the back, Tacos is toying with his phone, swiping right on some girls on a dating app, then he farts and puts his phone away. We're headed for Place de Stalingrad — "Stalincrack", to those in the know — the meeting place for half the junkies in Paris. Having never lived in Paris before being posted to the I3P, I know the area only by reputation.

The crew pile out of the van and split into two groups — in a technique called a pincer movement to corner dealers, as I'll later discover. I follow my colleagues across a small footbridge, walking quickly as they slip on their black gloves. I try to feel a sense of excitement, but the truth is, I'm scared shitless.

As we approach one of the little hills surrounding the Place de Stalingrad, we see nebulous shadows framed against the dawn light. Ghosts, zombies fucked up on crack — a cocaine derivative that sells for twenty to thirty euros a rock.

"Hey, look, over there — a *modou*. You can tell because he's better dressed than the rest of them."

Modou? What the hell does that mean? Tacos is

nodding to a fat Black guy wearing cargo pants with multiple pockets. We walk over to him.

"So, what are you doing here at this time of the morning?" Tacos asks.

"Me? I'm heading to work," the guy says.

"Yeah, yeah, you think I'm an idiot?"

I'm astonished by Tacos' confidence. As far as he's concerned, the guy's a dealer, no question. I'm trying to work out how he can be so sure.

Tacos frisks him; the putative dealer has no crack on him, but he does have two phones — a state-of-the-art smartphone and a cheap old-fashioned clamshell. In another pocket, he has about fifty euros in coins.

"I know you're a dealer," Tacos says menacingly. "OK, so maybe I can't cuff you this time, but I'll get you next time."

I stay in the background and watch. A couple of hours later, a Google search tells me that *modou* — from the Wolof language, meaning a "small trader" — is slang for a crack dealer. I wouldn't know a rock of crack if I found it in my pocket.

The suspect casually lopes away. Around us, there are only a handful of junkies left.

"Go on, time to go, we don't want your kind round here," shouts Tacos.

The three other officers are walking towards us from the far side of the square. They have made no arrests, simply having told a group of crackheads to move on.

The three junkies drag their emaciated carcasses, gaunt cheeks, and tattered clothes a little further off. They are sheltering under the arcades that line the square, seemingly waiting for us to leave.

The six of us climb back into the "TC", the callsign for a police van — "T because every call sign starts with T, and C for *camion*, a van. I'm in the back, sitting on a ripped black plastic bench.

Sitting next to me, Tacos is once again staring at Tinder, swiping right.

We drive through the silent deserted streets. At 7 am on a Tuesday, there is nothing much going on.

When out on patrol, every officer is issued with a radio set to the local police frequency. At any given moment, only one or two are turned on, so as not to drain the batteries. Only the team leader has his radio on constantly, so he can be contacted at any time. The radios connect to TN19, the local control station, which assigns missions to the various patrol cars.

TN19, the nerve centre of the commissariat, issues orders from an office on the second floor. The three uniformed officers there are constantly scanning CCTV footage of the streets on four flat-screen monitors. They can flick between every CCTV camera in the city, scanning for faces, for vehicles. TN19 also takes emergency calls, and can send patrol cars to an address.

Right now, we haven't been assigned a mission, so we drive aimlessly around the area. Tacos drools over "one last pair of tits" before putting his phone away. The riot shields and the orange-and-white traffic cones roll around on the floor of the van. Our TC is a rusty heap of junk with an engine that still happens to work.

"Hey, why don't we have a word with the guys at Police Judiciaire down on the Quai des Orfèvres?" Tacos suggests.

Two days earlier, an ADS had accidentally killed an officer in the new Police Judiciaire headquarters on the rue du Bastion, near the Porte de Clichy. They were messing around, playing quick-draw with their service pistols, when the ADS accidentally shot his colleague in the head.

"Any more news stories like that, and they'll take our guns away," says Tacos. "But the day they do that, there'll be fucking chaos. The scum out there know we're not allowed to fire at will, but at least the guns are a deterrent. If they take them away, we'll be up to our arses in armed robberies."

We pull up near the canal where immigrants sleep in cardboard boxes to shelter from the wind.

"TN19 to PS Alpha."

PS Alpha is the codesign for our patrol. TN19 has a mission for us.

"PS Alpha receiving," says Bison.

"Possible domestic abuse. A neighbour heard screaming. Can you check it out …? Third-floor apartment, 36, rue Barbanègre. The door code is 1234."

"Received. We're on our way."

Once inside the building, we knock on the door of the apartment where the screams were heard. A woman answers. She tells us that her ex-boyfriend has hidden her phone, that he's in there with her, that he's jealous because she has been seeing other guys, and that he's just spent the night her. We step inside, and four of my colleagues surround the man. He flashes us a dirty look.

The man allows the officers to search him, while the woman unleashes a torrent of abuse. Sheepish and a little scared, I stand behind Tacos. I'm taking no risks. Tacos is a big guy; he'll step in if he's needed. Having searched the man and his belongings, there is no sign of a missing phone. Meanwhile, Tacos talks to the woman and discovers that the lease on the apartment is in her name only. He passes this information to Bison.

"Alright, monsieur, since your name is not on the lease, we must ask you to leave the premises immediately," says the Captain.

The man picks up a bag of clothes and walks down the three flights of stairs with us. The police van starts up again.

"PS Alpha to TN19," says Bison.

"TN19 receiving."

"We've just left 36, rue Barbanègre. There was no sign of an assault, but since the lease on the apartment is in the woman's name, we instructed the man to leave the premises. No further action required."

"Noted. Thank you, PS Alpha."

Bison puts the radio down and turns to us.

"Anyone hungry? Shall we take a break?"

"Sure, if you like," says Tacos.

"PS Alpha to TN19."

"TN19 receiving, over."

"Permission to take a Whiskey Charlie break."

The Captain has requested a "WC" break. He uses the international phonetic alphabet used by police, firefighters, and the gendarmerie. It's usually used to communicate names or licence-plate numbers. At the academy, we had to learn it by heart: *Alpha, Bravo, Charlie, Delta, Echo* … I mentally recite the words. When I reach the letter O, I can't remember — what is it? Oscar? — I don't know anymore, I've forgotten.

"OK, fine," says the officer at TN19 Central.

The van pulls in to the police station garage. It is 8.00 am. Bison takes out an e-cigarette. I fish out a pack of smokes and a lighter.

Bison is a chatty guy. Forty-something, five foot seven, cropped greying hair, he is a Sous-Brigadier. His puny physique masks a nervous man. Bison never wanted to be a Brigadier, the highest rank among ordinary officers.

"I'm not interested in ranks. The reason I'm a cop is to piss off the bastards who piss off ordinary people. I don't really give a toss about the legal side. Or dealers either. But fuck with other people, and you'll have me to answer to."

Bison holds the honorary title of brigade leader. He is the oldest of the regular officers. While he vapes, he and another cop discuss the merits of the latest e-cigarette on the market.

"So, you're the new guy?" He flashes me a smile. "I'm Diego, but everyone calls me Mano."

Later, I'll find out that his nickname refers to the "hand of God" goal scored by Diego Maradona. Because in Spanish, "mano" means "hand".

"Hey. I'm Valentin."

"Are you thinking of applying for the regular police?"

This was one of the questions I anticipated when I first set foot in the commissariat. Spending fifteen months driving lunatics around without even applying to be in the regular force might seem strange: nobody wants to be an ADS forever.

"Not just yet. I wanted to join the brigade, wear out some shoe leather before I do."

"You'll learn a lot from us," he says, dragging on his plastic cigarette.

A cloud of white smoke explodes against the ceiling of the garage.

"Hey, have you done the IR for Monsieur and Madame?" Bison shouts.

"Oh no — *shit!* — I'll do it now," a voice calls back.

"IR" stands for "incident report", the official record of missions carried out during a shift. I follow Tacos into the office. He sits at a computer and launches the MCI,

the daybook software, and writes a short, formal text —
"short and sweet" — summarising what happened.

Forty-five minutes later, as we are driving around the
city again, we get a call from TN19 telling us to go back
to 36, rue Barbanègre. This time, the woman is alone.
She tells us that her ex came back, kicked in her front
door, and beat her. She wants to file a complaint. We
take her downstairs and search the surrounding area.
We're not likely to catch her attacker.

The woman sits next to me, in the back of the police
van. Tacos tells her to have the locks on her front door
changed and to stay with a family member for a while.

"PS Alpha to TN19," says Bison.

"TN19 receiving."

"We are bringing the victim to the commissariat to
file a complaint."

When we reach the rue Erik-Satie, the woman
gets out and goes to sit on one of the metal chairs in
the lobby, waiting to press charges. We go back out on
patrol.

"I swear, they get on my wick with their African
bullshit," Tacos mutters through gritted teeth.

20

I slide my orange key into the machine and get a piss-weak cup of coffee. Today, I'm going out with the PSZ — the Priority Security Zone squad. The PSZ was originally set up in the nineteenth arrondissement in 2012 to deal with crack dealers and violent robberies in the area between Stalingrad and the rue Riquet. These days, the squad can be called out to anywhere in the district. Our driver today is Xavier. Bison will be squad leader. I feel crushed by the weight of the bulletproof vest. I go down to the garage, where I find Bison and Mano.

"Steph asked me to run interference," Bison is telling his colleague. "We're going to do a little papering in a street full of bastards."

I'm beginning to realise that the word "bastard" generally refers to a young man, usually Black or Arab. More often than not, an immigrant.

"Steph is one of the Brigadiers-Chefs," says mano, seeing my puzzled look. "And 'paper' means fines. You know, parking tickets."

The most common approach, he explains, is to

punch the number plate of a vehicle parked on a double yellow line or in a loading bay into a special piece of police software, and issue the ticket.

"Do what your brigade leader asks, and they're more likely to be accommodating," says Bison. "Like, if you need a day off, for example."

I had no idea that cops could issue tickets. I thought that was only municipal parking attendants — who these days are called Public Highway Surveillance Agents.

In the commissariat, Bullitt seems overexcited; he's pacing around and shouting.

"We're going on a car hunt. There will be blood!"

"Are the top brass pushing for us to issue more tickets?" I ask.

"You've got a quota. Every month, senior officers can tell how many you've issued. But it doesn't add anything to your pay — if it did, I'd spend all day issuing fines. But they still expect us to crank up the numbers. 'MADs', papers ..."

MAD stands for *mise à disposition*, taking a suspect in for questioning. I've even heard officers use it as a verb: "to MAD".

"They're forever busting our balls over stats and numbers," says Bison. "Personally, I'm an old-school cop. These days, if you catch some snotty kid, you have to haul them in for questioning. Problem is, the kid just goes out and brags to his mates about being in custody.

Now, if I catch a kid carrying something, I just give him a slap. Slap him in front of his mates, and he doesn't feel like such a tough guy."

Bison tells me that before becoming an officer in the emergency services, he worked for the local police in Pontoise out in the suburbs; after that, he did stints with various departments of the Police Nationale. He moves around a lot — from being a cop on a bike, to a squad leader, to various other departments. He hasn't really decided what he wants.

"Whether we were in Pontoise or in Paris, we'd just pull into parking garage, ask a resident to let us into the apartment building, and beat the shit out of the local thugs," he crows.

"You didn't bring them in for questioning?"

"Fuck, no. You can't take a guy into custody if you've just knocked him into the middle of next week. The kid will be sent to a police doctor, and you'll get it in the arse. Back in the day, we'd regularly go round to 19, rue de Meaux, and give the little hoods a good hiding. These days, it's the other way around, they're not scared of cops any more. But back then, I swear, we had them shitting bricks."

I try to follow this logic: violate procedure by beating and terrorising young offenders. He fishes his phone out of his pocket and shows me a video.

"Here, this is one time I shot a little bastard who tried to rush me."

In the video, a guy with no helmet is riding a moped straight at Bison. I hear a bang. Bison only fires a single shot, but it is enough to injure the rider. By the end of the video, the moped is lying on the ground, and the guy is writhing in pain. I stare, wide-eyed. Bison tells me what happened next. The kid suffered serious injuries, and Bison was summoned to appear before the General Inspectorate of the National Police, the IGPN. He was interviewed several times about his use of a weapon during the incident. In the end, the IGPN concluded that he acted in self-defence.

"When was this?" I ask.

"Back in 2008."

Why has Bison still got the video on his phone ten years after the incident? Why show it to me like it's a video of his baby taking his first steps?

"If you're not allowed to fight back, to get down and dirty, it's not worth the effort," he says.

I am not able to "get down and dirty". The last time I was in a fight, I just took the punches. That was five years ago. I was drunk, and climbed onto the roof of a car when I came out of a bar. Three guys smashed my face in, and stole my wallet and my phone. End of story.

I don't mention this little episode to Bison. Much less that, ever since, at the first sign of trouble, I run like a rat up a drainpipe.

21

"I need go to the bog!" shouts one of the prisoners in custody.

"Yeah, yeah, I'm coming."

I go over to the bench, pick up a bunch of keys, and escort the prisoner to the toilets. Today, I'm working with Xavier monitoring the prisoners in custody. Xavier does not say a word; he keeps his nose in a pile of paperwork. Xavier used to be a soldier, but that is the only thing I know about him.

The prisoner in question is in cell C2, the second cell. The heels of my boots clack down the hallway. There is an overwhelming stench of piss.

I turn the large brass key in the lock and shoot back the latches on the metal door. Aside from the guy who is bursting for a piss, there are five minors asleep in a cell measuring nine by nine feet. Three are sharing the two makeshift mattresses and orange blankets. The other two are curled up on the concrete bench.

"Down to the end, turn right," I tell the prisoner.

There are three custody cells on the ground floor,

each of which can hold six people, plus two more cells
for drunks who are drying out.

The guy shuffles back from the toilets.

"What time is it?"

"Five past seven."

"What time's breakfast?"

"No idea. I'll check."

He goes back into the cell. I shoot home the bolts.

"Hey, Xav, what time is breakfast?"

"When everyone's awake — usually half past eight
or nine o'clock."

"Where do we get the food from?"

"You'll find juice boxes and packs of biscuits in the
cupboard at the back of the cell we use for searches."

He carries on filling out spreadsheets. I sit behind
the bench and stare at the monitor that shows footage
from the custody cells. From the motionless white
shapes I can make out against the black background, it
looks like everyone is still asleep. It is eerily quiet. Even
Bullitt, the duty sergeant, is silent.

A group of officers have been tasked with retrieving
a vehicle from a garage that won't open until 8.00 am.
In the meantime, some are standing around drinking
coffee, while the others are crowded around the bench,
laughing and watching porn on the police computers.

A little way off, a cop with a hipster haircut is
looking online for a new apartment. He's just split up
with his girlfriend. He doesn't want to live in central

Paris, and is looking for somewhere in the suburbs, in Seine-Saint-Denis or Val-de-Marne. Some of the other officers suggest names I've never heard of — places that are far outside the city.

"Hey, why don't you come live where I live, Ludo," says a female officer, flashing him a smile. "It's great, really quiet — there's practically no one there under sixty!"

The prisoners in the custody cells are starting to wake up. So begins the morning rush hour: some want to go to the toilet; others want their breakfast. I busy myself escorting people between the cells and the toilets while Xavier hands out breakfast. Being custody supervisor is like being a hotel manager, or a leader at a summer camp.

"Hey, Valentin, give me a hand here, we need to take away the mattresses," says Xavier.

We walk along the hallway, eyes fixed on the cells.

"Go on, you drag out the mattresses and blankets."

Some of the prisoners start complaining.

"But they let us keep them yesterday. Go on, officer, give us a break."

"That was yesterday. My instructions are that bedding is to be removed at 9.00 am."

"You can't expect us to just curl up on the floor, we're not dogs."

"You can all squeeze onto the bench there. If you want a comfy mattress, then maybe stop pulling this shit."

The prisoners continue to protest. In cell C1, the guy sprawled on the mattress refuses to give it back. Xavier simply whips it out from under him, dragging the guy a few yards as he pulls it out of the cell. The prisoner scrabbles to his feet and lumbers towards him menacingly. Xavier puts him in a choke hold and slams him against the wall. Panicked, I instinctively kick the cell door closed to stop the others from making a break for it.

Several other cops come running, with Bullitt leading the charge. He grabs the guy and takes him to the search room. The guy is looking sheepish now as Bullitt whips out his telescopic truncheon. He stares the prisoner straight in the eye, clearly prepared to hit him.

"Are you done? Have I made myself clear? I don't want to hear a peep out of you. Just keep your hole shut."

The man nods. Bullitt brings him back to his cell before bellowing down the hallway: "We take the mattresses away because we're not running a bloody hotel here!"

No one in the cells says another word. Xavier and I go back to our post. A plain-clothes officer appears.

"We need to take three of the juveniles out — one of the public prosecutors wants to talk to them by videolink. One of you will have to come up to the third floor with me. Standard security measures. One officer is not enough to escort three uncuffed prisoners."

I volunteer to go. Upstairs, we wait for a call from

the prosecutor. The three juveniles are chatting among themselves; they're all about fifteen or sixteen. One of them turns to me, a half-smile visible beneath his shock of blond hair.

"Monsieur, why did you join the police?"

I say nothing. The other boys giggle. I can see that one of them has braces on his teeth. The bottle-blond kid is still showing off for his mates.

"M'sieur, is it 'cos you were bullied in primary school?"

The other two burst out laughing.

"*Wallah*, don't talk to him, bro," say one of them.

I still don't answer. The plain-clothes cop leads us into the interview room, clearly annoyed. We've been waiting for the prosecutor for more than twenty minutes.

"I suppose you're going to turn on the tears, yeah? Tell him the cops are being mean to you, that it?" the plain-clothes cop taunts them.

"One of them hit me. I could press charges," says the first.

"When they were chasing me, they called me Bamboula," says another. "That's racist. I'm still in shock."

I leave the room and wait outside. Twenty minutes later, the three boys come out of the room. The prosecutor has decided to refer the case to court. They will be immediately escorted to the Paris Courthouse.

The three are still giggling; they don't seem concerned. I take them back to their cell.

While they are there, I search through their belongings in the evidence locker. In the rucksacks, I find folders and homework. One of the boys is in college; the other two are in secondary school.

Gradually, the cells begin to empty out. Then a squad arrives; they have been out MAD-ing. A young Algerian lad has been arrested for stealing a phone from a mother who was walking down the street with her two children. With his big hands, Toto handcuffs him to the bench. When Bullitt hears why the boy has been arrested, he jumps to his feet and marches over to him.

"I've had it up to the back teeth with kids like you!"

He lashes out, a vicious slap that leaves the sunken-eyed boy rubbing his cheek.

"Kids like you would be better off dead!" Bullitt growls, and then slaps the boy again, in front of the other officers. As before, no one turns a hair.

"I don't know why I bother," says Bullitt. "He'll be back on the streets by tomorrow — that's what always happens. You get kids like that being brought in twenty times a month, and they never get punished. They're victims of society."

22

This morning, during roll-call, I study the youthful faces of my fellow officers. Four are mixed-race, two are Black, and two are Arab. The rest, like me, are white. At the police academy, all the ADS recruits were white. Even here, we are the overwhelming majority.

A latecomer tiptoes in at the back. Just in time. A skinny guy I spotted a few days earlier, he has an air of quiet strength that I find striking. I really want to talk to him, but I can't do that right now. He keeps to the sidelines and does not seem very talkative.

His name is Stan. We chatted once, while I was working as cell supervisor with Xavier. He and his team brought in a girl who had been the victim of domestic violence. Stan insisted that we give her something to eat. The same breakfast as for those in custody — a couple of biscuits and a carton of orange juice.

"At least she'll have eaten something," Stan said, looking at me with owl eyes that seemed too big for his thin face.

When roll-call is over, I take off my cap and slip it into a pocket.

I am watching Stan. He doesn't say hello to his colleagues. His expression is grave, inscrutable; his hair is cut short and parted on the left. I wander over to say hello.

"Hey, how are things?"

He shakes my hand, gives a curt answer, and walks away.

23

An old man of about seventy is sitting on the bed, dead. He didn't have time to lie down or even to take off his left sock. His heart stopped while he sat there, fully clothed, his head resting against the headboard. I stand in the doorway and survey the room. The dead man's mouth and eyes are wide open. Four of us have just arrived on the scene — Benjamin, Fanny, Ludo the bearded hipster, and me.

The man lived alone. His carer raised the alarm when she discovered that the door was locked from the inside. Firefighters broke down the patio doors in the living room to get inside, discovered the body, and contacted us. The call sign for our missions is "Delta Charlie Delta". "DCD" in French is pronounced *décédé* — dead.

The apartment is clean and tidy; two cats are cowering behind the bedroom curtains. Benjamin, the team leader, radios in.

"Dead in bed. Seated. Age, approximately seventy, likely by natural causes due to underlying health issues.

A number of medications on table next to the sofa. I don't have the details yet."

The first priority is to identify the dead man. We look around, and I find his ID card lying on the floor by the sofa. I hand it to Benjamin.

"I was pretty close, as it goes, he's actually seventy-one. He obviously liked his food," the squad leader says, going through the kitchen cupboards. "Pork, sauerkraut, tripe, steak, ham, croque-monsieur, baguette, mashed potatoes."

We stand for a few minutes before the lifeless body. We study the old man. And comment.

"He's in pretty good shape, all things considered, steady on his feet," Sabrina says ironically.

"His fingers are starting to go black," says Ludo.

"But if no one's seen him for a week, his family can't have been too worried."

Fanny wonders aloud whether the cats would have started to eat the corpse if it had not been found. People start recounting their most grisly experiences: a drowned man, a hanging corpse, a man found dead on his toilet.

Benjamin has just found a sheaf of medical records, and is on the radio.

"He was clinically obese, had had a pulmonary embolism, acute heart failure, and gout."

"In that case, he's well out of it. I mean, with all that lot, he's costing the health service too much money," Ludo laughs.

An OPJ — a forensic officer — arrives an hour later. He takes photos of the deceased, then sketches the position of the body and writes a brief description. It's official. Natural causes. Routine.

We wait another two hours. Just before 6.30 pm, three guys from the undertakers show up to take away the body. The three heavyset men pick up the corpse and slide it into a body bag.

"I have to say, it's not as exciting as *CSI* or *NCIS*," says Benjamin.

24

Today is my first day behind the wheel of a police vehicle. Despite the fact that I've had a driving licence for more than a decade, I feel nervous — worried about what my fellow officers will think of my driving skills, terrified of reversing into a parking space, or, worse, pranging another car.

I am driving the Major, the highest-ranking officer in our brigade. His name is Serge Pommier, but everyone just calls him "the Major". At forty-nine, Serge suffers from crippling back pain. He hobbles rather than walks, his torso skewed at a strange angle. Serge has served in our commissariat for twenty-five years, and describes himself as a confirmed bachelor. "No woman would have me, I'm too pigheaded," he says.

Emergency services broke down the door of an apartment in order to rescue a woman and take her to hospital, so we have sent a team to remain in the apartment until a locksmith arrives.

I park the Volkswagen E-Golf on the rue

d'Aubervilliers, and stay in the car to make sure no one vandalises it.

The Major has left his paperwork on the dashboard, so I leaf through the files just to kill time. Dozens of prefilled fines for street hawking. This is the Major's specialty. Each form reads: "Criminal offence, to wit: street hawking without a licence or permit, displaying and offering goods for sale or practising any profession in a public place in contravention of applicable laws and statutory provisions." Article 51 of a law passed in March 2011 further specifies that such offences are punishable by a term of imprisonment of six months and a fine of 3,750 euros. "Individuals found guilty of such offences may incur additional penalties, including the seizure and destruction of any goods or chattels implicated in the offence."

Once the locksmith has done his work, the squad comes to join in. Our target now is street hawkers. The Major knows precisely where to find the pedlars scattered throughout the district. On the fringes of the markets at Belleville and Joinville, on the rue Curial, the rue Mathis, sometimes at the tram stop at Porte de la Villette — and this is where he tells me to drive.

Less than a minute after climbing out of the Golf, he has spotted his first victim.

"Alim, I've already told you a hundred times you can't sell here. Next time, I'm hauling you in," he says to one of his regulars, a Bengali peanut-seller, before confiscating the merchandise and the steel roasting pan. Ludo carts the stuff away.

"It's really fucking embarrassing having to do this kind of thing in front of people," says Ludo, a little disappointed.

"The reason I target street hawkers is to crack down on trafficking," growls the Major.

We pile back into the vehicle, and I have only just driven around the corner when the Major tells me to pull over. This time, he issues a spot fine to an Indian man selling fruit and vegetables. Ludo goes with him, just in case. Protocol insists that no officer be alone on a public street.

Four wooden crates of melons, bananas, and mandarins are loaded into the boot of the vehicle.

"I can't see that these guys are doing anything wrong," I say to the Major.

"You don't get it. Regular market traders have to pay for their pitch. These guys don't pay for a pitch, they don't pay market taxes, they don't pay taxes, and they're getting unemployment benefits. So it's hardly surprising that market traders who have to get up at four o'clock every morning are justifiably pissed off at this kind of competition."

I nod.

"That's why we shut them down. To say nothing of the fact that most of them don't even have residence permits."

• • •

We head back to the police station to unload our haul. In theory, all confiscated goods must be destroyed. In practice, the fruit and vegetables are usually left in dumpbins in the garage for cops to take home. Some officers help themselves; others turn up their noses — "You've no idea where this stuff has been". From time to time, we seize cartons of contraband cigarettes. At the end of the month, when I'm running short of funds, I'll sometimes take a couple of packs. It's contraband, but it's free. Some of my fellow officers who are short on cash also smoke these foul cigarettes.

Where is the Major? No one seems to know, so we hang around outside the commissariat, waiting.

"So, what did you get up to this morning?" the rookie cop on duty asks Ludo.

Ludo pretends to rack his brains for a long minute, then says: "So … We issued some fines … Then, at some point, I think we issued fines, and after that I'm pretty sure we issued some fines."

Ludo laughs as he twirls his *tonfa* — slang for a side-handle police baton.

The Major reappears, his shirt only half-tucked into his trousers.

"I was on Vetipol. It's such a bloody hassle ordering new uniforms."

So, while we were twiddling our thumbs outside

the commissariat, the Major was buying socks on the official website that sells police-issue clothes.

We set off again, and the Major seems determined to carry on issuing fines. Ten minutes later, we stop another Bengali man, who is selling fresh mint outside a market. The Major asks to see his permit. The man doesn't have one. Running his name through the database, the Major finds out that the hawker is on the national sex offenders' register — what we call Fichier Judiciaire Automatisé des Auteurs d'Infractions Sexuelles (FIJAIS) — which "lists all adults or juveniles who have been convicted of sexual assault". As a result of his conviction, the Bengali man is summoned to appear once a year before a judge.

"I bet you had an eye for a pretty girl, huh, you old perv!" says the Major.

The man says nothing, though he seems to understand. The Major issues him with a fine, then turns to me.

"You, load up the crates."

I pile four crates of fresh mint into the boot. The trader walks away, stuffing the ticket into his pocket. I start the car.

"So, is he an illegal immigrant?" I ask.

"Yeah. But he can't be deported. Anyone who is the subject of an ongoing criminal investigation can't be deported."

"Is this about the sexual offences?"

"Yeah. It looks as though he might have been part of a ring grooming young girls. These bastards are capable of anything."

"Right, that's one more MAD," says the Major, with a satisfied smirk.

And this is his rationalisation for the flurry of fines and tickets. Each one counts as an arrest. Every fine issued to a street hawker boosts the figures.

"So, how many MADs do we issue a month?" I ask.

"No idea, it depends … This month, it must be close to seventy-five."

"So, how does it work, is there a minimum quota?

"As long as the figures aren't too low, no, there's no quota …"

"But there's a lot of competition between brigades?"

"Oh, yes."

"So, are we trailing behind the other squads in our commissariat?"

"No, no, we're way ahead."

25

Standing in front of my locker, I change my clothes, preparing to once again become an anonymous citizen. I toss my police shirt into the locker, where it joins the hideous jumble of dirty clothes I've managed to pile up in a couple of months. I am a little more careful with my bulletproof, slipping it onto a hanger. A few lockers to my right, Loïc is taking off his belt and his shoes.

"We did fuck-all this morning. The Alpha is the only one who notched up an arrest."

"Yeah, I heard something about it on the radio. What was it again?"

"We stopped a car and questioned a bunch of guys. Turns out they had a sword stashed in the car — a huge, vicious thing. They also had a knife, a crowbar, a balaclava, and a fucking bulletproof vest. Standard-issue bastard gear."

The "bastards" in question were promptly arrested. Another MAD.

"The rest of us did bugger-all. Apart from a couple of tramps and a bunch of junkies, that was it."

Most of my fellow officers find this thankless work, and I'm starting to find it boring — petty duties intended for a "toy cops". No one here signed up for this kind of drudge work; they want callouts that get their adrenaline pumping: catching fleeing suspects, manning road checks. And, if at all possible, making arrests.

"Have you been at the station long?" I ask Loïc.

"No, only a couple of months. I'm still a rookie."

I forgot that there is only one stripe on his uniform, which means that he's not yet a fully fledged officer. He's what older officers call a "probie", "small fry". After a year in the force, he will get a second stripe, making him a full officer.

"What did you do before?"

"I worked for Sephora."

"The perfume shop?"

"Yeah. I hated it. I've wanted to apply for the force for a long time."

I step out of the commissariat, slip on my headphones, and crank up Bashung's *La nuit je mens* at full volume. From Ourcq métro station, it takes about forty-five minutes for me to get home. I get out at Château de Vincennes and walk for seven minutes to my local supermarket. From the shelves of Franprix, I fill my basket with all the things that French gastronomy dismisses as junk food: pre-cooked sausages, cheese-filled chicken nuggets, a pack of crisps, a bottle of

Coke, and a bag of Haribo strawberry jellies for dessert. I intend to wash down this feast with liberal quantities of cigarettes and coffee.

It's 3.30 pm. when I turn the key in my apartment. I slump onto my faux-leather sofa. Every undercover mission is a test of endurance. There's still a long way to go. If I'm going to stick it out for six months, there are still four to come.

So far, my only contact with other officers has been limited to work. I'm finding it hard to adjust to their world. On previous undercover investigations, all I had to do was talk about football and I'd fit in right away. But in the force, no one really seems interested. "Football is for fags — someone only has to touch them and they're rolling on the pitch like drama queens", Mano says when I bring up the subject. So I'm still struggling to find something to talk about. They chat about *The Walking Dead*, a TV show I've never watched, and they obsess over cars, about which I know nothing.

While I reheat the sausages in the microwave, before dousing them with mustard, I check the calendar stuck over my desk with Blu-Tac. I mark the days I'm on duty, and the days I'm off. Right now, I haven't applied for any holiday leave because I'm worried I won't be there on the one day that it matters. Officers with the Police Secours in Paris work a four–two rota. Four days on, two days off. They call it a cycle. Morning shifts, then evening shifts. And so on.

As I wolf down the chicken nuggets, I watch some football on YouTube. I feel like doing nothing. Like taking a nap. But I still have to do my daily two hours of note-taking.

Sitting at my computer, I yawn as I run through the cases we dealt with this morning. Kicking homeless people out of shelters; dealing with a noise complaint; Bison taking us to a sex shop for fetishists to get tickets for a gig organised by the owner. While I wandered the aisle in full uniform, surrounded by whips, bondage gear, and dildos, he stood chatting to the boss. Then Bison insisted he wanted to get sandwiches from a bakery on the far side of Paris. The officer behind the wheel turned on the lights and sirens, and floored the accelerator, weaving between cars and buses that swerved to get out of the way, probably assuming we were on an urgent case. We ran red lights and mounted pavements, all just to get a couple of pâté sandwiches.

I finish taking notes. At about 10 pm, I drift off and sleep like a log.

At 4.25 am precisely, the alarm on my phone goes off. I groan into my pillow. I climb down from my bedroom on the mezzanine. A shower does nothing to erase the dark circles under my eyes. I'm completely shattered.

26

"Robbery in progress, Total petrol station, 152, boulevard de la Villette." The call comes over the radio. "Three individuals in balaclavas on the premises."

A robbery, only a few blocks away. The Major turns on the blues-and-twos. I put the pedal to the metal. My knuckles are white as I grip the steering wheel and we careen through central Paris at 120kph, running red lights, barely slowing for pedestrian crossings, weaving between cars. I give it everything I've got. Given that I'm no action man, I need to prove myself useful in some other way if I want to spend more time on the streets. By being a good driver, for example.

Sitting next to me, the Major frantically tries to catch the documents that were sent fluttering around the car when I made a hard-right turn. I nearly plough into a Mondeo. It's a close call. In the back seat, the two officers cling to the handles. The adrenaline rush of a potential arrest.

"Get the fuck out of the way!" Ludo roars at a car that is slow to pull over and let us pass.

The Total station appears on the right. I screech to a stop between the road and the parking bays.

"I hope they're armed," says Ludo, visibly excited at the prospect of a gun battle.

High on protein shakes and pumping iron, he leaps out of the car and sets off at a run, drawing his service revolver. By the time he reaches the petrol station, he's put ten yards between him and the female officer running behind. The Major shuffles rather than walks. He has no interest in such cases; he would rather be issuing fines.

I hang back. I feel like making a run for it. What if the three guys inside start shooting? We'll have to fire back. I rest my left hand on my service weapon as I run half-heartedly. I have no choice but to follow, but I'm in no hurry. I'm not about to take a bullet in the belly for the sake of a book. Ludo reaches the glass doors. The place is locked up.

"Forget it, there's no one in there," Ludo grumbles. "They just shattered the windows — look, Major, there's glass shards everywhere."

"What do you think they did it with?" asks the female officer. "Truncheons?"

"Probably just batons," says the Major.

"Major to TN19 Central," the Major barks into his radio. "We've arrived at the scene, boulevard de la Villette. Suspects made a failed attempt to enter. There's no one inside. We are leaving the scene."

I activate the central locking on the Golf.

27

"Hey, Toto, are we playing football during the next cycle or not?" a fellow officer calls across the changing room.

"No idea."

Football? I've got a colleague in the commissariat who plays football. I edge my way into the conversation.

"I'd be up for a game."

"Oh really, d'you play? Cool. I'll add you to the WhatsApp group. And the brigade group, while I'm at it. What's your phone number?"

28

Some cop posts a YouTube video to the brigade's WhatsApp group. The headline reads: "May 1: Riot officer caught hurling a paving slab".

Tacos: I don't see the problem, looks like reasonable force to me ☺☺☺

Bullitt: Too right!!!! Hey, the guy just blew a fuse LOL.

Another officer: We need to show people the decent work done by cops, the media are always on the lookout for police cock-ups.

Toto: Those fucking anarchists were shitting themselves!! It's more fun when you let the dogs out!! ☺

Tacos: ☺☺ + drooling smiley[8]

Another officer posts a link to an article in the *Le Parisien* with the headline "Did Police Officer Shove Baton Down Demonstrator's Trousers? The General Inspectorate Investigates".

Tacos: Huh. Fucking bullshit question.

Vargo: We were told: not down the trousers.

Tacos: I didn't see anything, I had my back turned, sorry I can't help with the internal investigation.

Vargo: The investigation will be quickly done and dusted. The officer was trying to slide his baton into the demonstrator's belt so he could pull him out of the crowd. That's all ... End of investigation, no further action.

Tacos: Cool.

Bullitt: Jesus, it's crazy this mongoloid country.

Tacos: Yep.

Bullitt: Reading the comments makes me crazy. Bunch of fucking faggots.

Vargo: Yeah, they're sick in the head ... We should show them what Paris would be like with no police for a week.

29

I'm working with Stan for the first time; we're on custody-cell supervision. It's only 8.15 am. To get a bit of peace so that I can chat to him, I suggest handing out breakfast early.

"Time enough for that later," says my colleague. "They're bastards, let 'em wait."

Okay. He makes the decisions. Stan gets himself a snack — steamed vegetables and a smoothie. The guy doesn't drink and doesn't smoke. I've spotted a pair of boxing gloves hanging in his locker. I wouldn't like to find myself face to face with him in the ring.

Since the place is deserted and the nine custody prisoners are all asleep, he takes an interest in me: "How are things? Are you managing to settle in?"

"Yeah, yeah." I flash an embarrassed smile. "What about you, how long have you been working here?"

"Two and a half years. Before that, I was an ADS. I was lucky, I was posted to the CS.[9] It was really tough at first, but I made a bunch of really solid arrests. When I first joined the brigade here, with a bunch of guys who've moved on now, we used to do real work. These days, it's gone to the dogs."

"How do you mean?"

"There are too many cops who can't be arsed to do anything."

Stan sighs.

"Look, I make no distinction between ADS guys like you and regular officers. But the ADS officers working here drew the short straw. It's just mindless chores."

He reels off the skills of an officer cop we call "the Prof" — an articulate guy who strikes me as having a good grasp of psychology.

"He's a good cop, but he doesn't belong in the brigade. Then again, he's clever and he knows the procedure inside out."

He runs through some of the other officers. Stan is a tough critic. Very few of our colleagues are up to his standards. "When he retires, he'll do one of two things," he comments about another officer. "He'll either put a bullet in his brain, or he'll show up here every day to piss us off."

In one of the custody cells, some guy starts shouting: "Let your soul express itself! Free your mind! It is an achievement. Suicide is good! I'm a police officer, I should kill myself. That is my purpose. Suicide is good!"

"Me, I did vocational courses at school," says Stan. "When I started out, I was shifting boxes in Leclerc warehouses; my grandfather got me the job."

Then he talks about working for a landscape gardener.

"He hired me on a trial basis, and four months later, when he saw I was up to the job, he gave me a full-time gig."

Stan is the only member of the brigade who grew up in Paris. In all likelihood he'll stay here, since there are more police stations in the capital than anywhere else.

"Free yourself! Suicide is good!" the guy in the cell shouts again.

"What's he in for?" I ask.

"Incitement to terrorism, I think ... But we can't do anything, he's not one of ours."

Meaning: he was arrested by officers from another district who brought this lunatic here because their custody cells were overcrowded.

"Kill yourself! It's okay to kill yourself. Suicide will set you free. Repeat after me. It is a culmination for you. Your goal is suicide, policemen. Suicide is good!"

This guy is driving me crazy, but Stan goes on, completely unflustered.

"Before, I wasn't a big fan of the police; actually, I couldn't stomach them."

A plain-clothes detective appears to retrieve the garrulous prisoner. Stan hands her the keys to the custody cells. The prisoner is an Arab guy of average height with a receding hairline. He can't be more than thirty. Stan glares at him.

"I have to say, I'm disappointed. I expected a war machine."

The prophet of suicide does not utter another word. He remains sheepish in the face of Stan's defiant stare.

"Later, I got the idea of becoming a cop into my head," Stan says. "And then I saw a poster that said the police were recruiting."

So he applied to be an ADS, and later applied to be a regular officer. Having now spent two and a half years here, he's one of the longest-serving members of the brigade. But he wants to work somewhere else.

"I'm done with this place, I'm sick and tired of it. I've got nothing left to prove here. I know I'm good, so I'm hoping to transfer to the BSG."

BSG stands for the Brigade de Soutien de Quartier (Neighbourhood Support Brigade) — heavyset guys in blue overalls. The next step up from a simple brigade cop. No drudge work there, it's all arrests and guaranteed adrenaline rushes. The BSG respond to incidents of urban violence — "UV" in police jargon — such as clashes between rival gangs. Next to him, I feel like a plastic cop.

In the custody cells, there are two guys in their twenties who were arrested at a *gilets jaunes* protest yesterday. They're accused of being "black bloc anarchists". The officers who arrested them were thrilled at the idea they'd nabbed a couple of black blocs, then gobsmacked to discover that the both of the guys are cadets de la République — a police rank close to that of ADS. The notion of cops turning into rioters makes them uneasy.

Bullitt, just back from an arrest, takes over the case and leads one of them into an interrogation room.

"So you're the member of the black bloc?"

The suspect mumbles, clearly intimidated. In his gravelly voice, Bullitt roars: "Listen, we're just as pissed off about the situation as you are. We don't like the Macron government any more than you do. But do you really think the solution is to smash things up? To steal and loot? How would you like it if someone robbed your place? Do you really think that destroying this is the solution?"

After a long exchange, Bullitt comes out.

"Another fucking middle-class boy trying to annoy his parents. I swear, the kid's got a screw loose. He said he enjoys smashing the system."

This suspect is scheduled to be referred to hospital later this morning. He suffers from Wilson's disease, a rare genetic disorder caused by a build-up of copper in the body.

"Better hope he doesn't run into a gang of Travellers," quips an officer.

Everyone laughs. Everyone except Stan, who doesn't seem to share his fellow officer's prejudices about the travelling community stripping copper piping from vacant houses. Or maybe he's too engrossed in the game he's just downloaded on his phone. Stan told me what it's called, but I've already forgotten. Like me, he's bored.

At 2 pm, I head down to the changing rooms. For the past week, we've had to change in the dark because the rickety fluorescent light still hasn't been repaired. Toto is angry.

"There are some shithole police stations in the country, but this dump … I swear," he says. "So, what were up to, big guy?

"Cell supervision with Stan."

Toto pulls a face.

"That guy? He thinks he's a headcase, though he hasn't even been here all that long. He's an arrogant tosser."

"How so?"

"He makes out like he's this great hunter. A hunter is a cop who has instinct, who can see things coming, who has flair. This guy does a lot of stop-and-searches, but that's about it. If I did eighteen stop-and-searches a day, I'd eventually stumble on a perp, too."

30

Bullitt: Did you see the piece in *Le Parisien*? The Paris public prosecutor says he's planning to charge the cop.
Benjamin: No, no, that's not what he said. Well, not just that.
Vargo: He's playing politics, he's trying to pacify the *gilets jaunes*.
Bullitt: WTF???? Of course he's trying to fuck over a cop. Have you lost the plot or what? We've got colleagues out there who could get it in the neck just because this son of a bitch is grovelling to the fucking *gilet jaunes* faggots.

Bullitt posts a screenshot of the article in question. "What will be decided about pending cases?" Bullitt has highlighted the prosecutor's response. "All police procedure will be carefully analysed. Many incidents will require no further action. However, we expect the actions of a number of officers to be referred to the criminal courts by the end of the year."

Bullitt: Personally, I don't think you can say stuff like that. Sounds like they've already decided to prosecute. Box-ticking fucking bullshit.

Benjamin: Yeah, but he also says that in lots of cases there will be no further action taken.

Bullitt: Great. Good for him. But maybe he should let the IGPN do their work before opening his big mouth. Fucking bastard.

Vargo: But they'll make examples of other people.

Bullitt: Like I said, a lot of cops are going to take this as political posturing. Look, I'm gonna stop now, otherwise I'll bust a blood vessel.

Vargo: I've gotta say, with all this shit, I don't understand why some cops bother taking along tear gas grenades and rubber bullets.

Bullitt: LOL.

31

"TN19 to TV Sierra."

"TN19 receiving," says Sabrina, the Sierra Patrol leader for the day.

"Noise complaint at 12, rue Compans. I repeat, 12, rue Compans — apparently a bunch of kids playing music. Could you check it out?"

"Roger. On our way."

Xavier, who is behind the wheel of a Renault Mégane, changes course and takes a road running perpendicular to the Canal de l'Ourcq. Sitting in the back seat next to me, Mano is already pulling on his gloves.

It's the first time I've been on the rue Compans, a narrow little street lined with grey buildings. It's mid-afternoon, and six boys of about fifteen or sixteen are hanging around listening to music. They're crowded together on the concrete forecourt outside the front door of an apartment building. One of the boys is holding up a black speaker that's blaring out some autotuned rap. A neighbour called to complain about the noise.

"Hey, I'm guessing you know why we're here?" Mano asks the boys as we climb out of the police car.

The teenagers' only answer is silent defiance.

"It's the music … There are neighbours complaining about the noise, so I want you to turn it off, right now."

The music is switched off, and Mano starts checking the kids over. He leads the interrogation. The kids line up against the grey wall. It's a routine stop-and-search.

Sabrina hangs back: a police officer is not permitted to perform a search on someone of the opposite sex. I frisk the guy holding the speaker. In a calm, authoritative voice, I reel off the orders.

"Empty your pockets! Take off the cap and turn it over!"

He does as he's told, refusing to look me in the eye or say a word.

"What's your name?"

"Konaté," he says, stone-faced.

"How old are you?"

"Sixteen."

I place my hands on his hips and then slide them up his chest to his shoulders. I pat his lower back, his arms, his legs down to his ankles. He's got nothing on him. No weed in his pockets, and no ID card either. Neither have the others.

Yet another callout with no result. We've had a string of them all afternoon, starting with a spat between neighbours over the loan of some tools, followed by a series of vehicle checks and some random stop-and-searches of people my colleagues thought looked suspicious. Every time, the result is "nothing to report" — "*rien à signaler*" in police lingo, or just "RAS" — or rather *RASSSS*, as Sabrina hisses into the radio. The noise complaint is just one more futile callout to add to an endless series.

I tuck my gloves back into in my trouser pocket, ready to climb into the back seat of the car.

Mano is still standing in front of the boys, sizing them up.

"I'm sick and tired of being called out for shit like this! Do you really think we've got nothing better to do? You kids are starting to seriously piss us off," he growls angrily.

His face is expressionless; he's playing the role of the bad cop giving a lecture. A grown-up cop facing down a bunch of fresh-faced teenagers.

But his attempt to instil fear doesn't work. The six boys don't seem remotely intimidated by our uniforms. They stand, staring at us. "We didn't do nothing," says Konaté, the kid I just searched.

Mano goes over and stands in front of the kid.

"What d'you say? I don't think I heard you," he says. He pats the kid's cheek.

"Hey, hey, back up! *Wallah*! Get your hands off me," says the boy. "Who do you think you are?"

Xavier and I stride over. He stops in front of the first

teenager, while Mano is still standing next to the kid with the baseball cap. I hang back and survey the scene with what I'm hoping is a cold, hard stare. Being back-up suits me, as long as things don't kick off.

"Go on then, *Wallah*," says Konaté, "I'll take you on, one on one."

Mano lashes out. A stinging slap across the boy's right cheek. Things have just kicked off.

"And anyway, you're piss-weak," says the kid. "You're not a real man."

The other five teens don't move a muscle.

Mano slaps the kid again.

"You little shit!"

"Yeah, yeah, shut yo' mouth," says the kid.

"Hey, shut it, bro, don't say nothing," one of his friends interjects.

Faced with a kid who is not about to back down, Mano completely loses it. He slaps hthe boy again, twice, three times, maybe four or five. Tensions are rising so fast, I forget to count the blows.

"Right," says Mano. "Let's take him in."

He makes the decision without consulting anyone. Since the kid doesn't have any ID on him, we can legitimately take him to the station to perform a simple ID check. Nobody quibbles. Mano bundles the boy into the back seat and sits next to him. I squeeze in next to them.

• • •

On the drive back to the commissariat, Mano lets rip. This time, they're not slaps — they're punches. How many? I've no idea, but I'm paralysed by the brutal scene. Konaté stifles a groan. In the heat of the arrest, Mano forgot to handcuff him, so the boy brings up his arms to protect his face, he struggles, and I grab hold of his hands to calm him. But Mano, who's now completely berserk, uses his elbow to pin the boy's chest so he can lay into him.

"Mano, ease up a little," Sabrina tries to calm him.

Mano doesn't hear. I try saying "Calm down". But it's useless.

Mano is completely out of control; he's laying into Konaté like a man possessed, and yelling things like "Shut your mouth, you little fucker!"

Xavier drives at full speed to the commissariat, sirens howling. I feel like I'm going crazy.

We get to the station and pull in; I help the kid get out of the car.

"Don't say a word, just do what you're told," I whisper some unwelcome advice. "And don't get riled up."

There's no way he won't be kept in custody.

When Konaté refuses to be handcuffed to the bench, Mano hits him again and forcibly restrains him. Two fat tears roll down the boy's cheeks. What's going through the mind of this sixteen-year-old, sobbing with helpless rage?

How can he ever trust the police again after this incident?

A few minutes later, he is presented to the officer empowered to make arrests, who takes down his details and offers to let him phone a lawyer and a relative, as protocol requires before he can be taken into custody. It is 5.40 pm, I've just witnessed a police fuck-up, and Konaté will spend the night in a police cell.

I mentally rewind to the beginning of the incident. It starts off innocuously. A mid-afternoon noise complaint. Teenage boys turn off their speaker. A frustrated cop bawls them out ("I'm sick and tired of being called out for shit like this"). A kid replies: "We didn't do nothing." The cop taps the kid on the cheek — a futile gesture in violation of protocol intended to deliberately humiliate the teenager in front of his friends. Out of pride, the kid responds to this physical threat with a verbal one ("I'll take you on, one on one"). Mano strikes the first blow, and even though the boy does not retaliate, Mano carries on hitting and insulting the teenager, then bundles him into the police car, where he punches him again and again. It's called a police cock-up. But a cock-up implies an incident that got out of hand, whereas I feel what I'd witnessed was an utterly unwarranted assault.

We could have confiscated the wireless speaker and left. Or said nothing and walked away. We could even have hauled the kid in for threatening behaviour (a moot point, since Mano made the first threat). Instead, Konaté was beaten up.

I feel that the most terrifying aspect of the entire incident was that I did nothing and, worse still, fellow officers who outrank me did not intervene. Because when it comes to blame, that is my only justification: I'm a nobody, a rookie, an ADS, the officer least qualified to question the action of a de facto "superior" officer.

Xavier and Mano spend the rest of the day sitting at a computer, writing up the incident report. They have to explain why the teenager was arrested. A little further off, Sabrina is chatting with some other officers. As squad leader, she doesn't have to worry about the report:

> Acting on the orders of the Commissaire Divisionnaire, a senior police officer having territorial jurisdiction in the nineteenth arrondissement, a squad was dispatched in a marked police vehicle with call sign TV Sierra. Those present were officers Garcia and Foucaud, together with ADS Gendrot. All officers were wearing regulation-issue uniforms with ranks and insignias clearly visible.

So much for the bureaucratic opening lines. It is Xavier who types the rest of the incident report, under the watchful eye of Mano. I'm sitting next to them, listening to their conversation. I quickly realise their ploy. They plan to blame Konaté and absolve Mano of all responsibility, insisting that he remained calm and professional throughout the incident, and did not act violently. They go so far as to cast Mano as the victim. It's insane.

Mano intends to file charges against the boy for threatening behaviour to a police officer.

"The suspect said that he was not afraid of us. We asked him to repeat what he had said, and at that point, he shouted: "Shut your mouth." Mano is dictating.

They still need to work out at what point the kid became violent.

"So, for the assault itself, we have to put that it occurred inside the police vehicle," says Xavier.

"What?" I interrupt. "When you started beating up the kid?" I say disingenuously, determined to make them face up to reality, even if only between ourselves.

"Uh … well, when we were forced to restrain him," Mano mutters, no doubt startled by my direct question.

"He's got a lump, a small swelling on his left side," adds Tacos, who is acting supervisor today and has just been to see Konaté in his cell.

"Right, we'll put that into the incident report," says Mano. "Anyway, who's to say that he didn't do it himself once he was in the cell? And besides, when I punched him back there, I hit him on the jaw. But if you're saying there's a swelling on his left side …"

Mano turns to me, expressionless.

"The kid's an arsehole. He should have kept his mouth shut."

"He's a kid, he was just showing off in front of his friends," I say.

But it's like talking to a brick wall.

"The thing is, we don't get called out to the Compans estate much these days. The Neighbourhood Support Group are the only ones working on the ground there. But they're all about surveillance, they don't do any stop-and-search, don't make any arrests. The whole estate is riddled with hard drugs. These kids, they're off their faces most of the time."

Behind the computer monitor, Xavier remains stone-faced. The incident report isn't finished; we will be in the office for a long time yet writing a report that bears no relationship to the facts.

"You could say that I used my arm to brace his head against the back of the seat to avoid … to avoid … problems," Mano mutters.

"What were you doing?" Xavier turns to me. "Didn't you restrain him?"

"I, uh … I held his arms."

"Right, put that. And you also need to put that the suspect was still threatening after we arrived at the station," Mano says.

He takes a tube of cheese-and-onion Pringles from his bag. He offers some to me. He also offers to make me a coffee. It's the first time anyone has offered to make me one.

32

Early afternoon the following day, I'm loitering outside the commissariat in my bulletproof vest, guarding the entrance to the station with a female officer. She is chatting to Sabrina, the duty sergeant, when Mano appears in the doorway. He about to go out on patrol, and is waiting for the rest of his crew.

"Shit ... the little fucker filed a complaint for police brutality," Mano whispers, his brow furrowed.

"You can hardly blame him ..." Sabrina glares at him, "that's what it was."

During the incident with Konaté, Sabrina was the squad leader. At the time, she did nothing to stop Mano. Now, in hindsight, she challenges him with the truth. Mano ignores her.

"So, that means you're going to be interviewed," he says to me.

"Interviewed?"

"Yeah, you're gonna be questioned about what happened yesterday."

•••

Things have suddenly taken a very different turn.

The kid has filed a complaint. An internal investigation is now in progress, so Xavier, Sabrina, and I, the three other officers on the patrol, will now have to be interviewed. Standard procedure. Under my blue cop's cap, I'm sweating about what I should do.

I could say that Mano insulted the kid and threw the first punch, that he completely lost control. That's what my conscience is telling me to do.

Then again, I'm just a rookie ADS, so in all likelihood, if I say that, I'll pay dearly. My chances of convincing the internal investigation inquiry are practically zero — all the other officers at the scene are senior to me, and all of them plan to back up Mano. Even Sabrina, our squad leader, intends to testify in his favour, despite just telling him to his face that she thinks it was police brutality. The unspoken rule is crystal clear: no matter what happens, we stick together.

Besides, if I tell the truth I know I'll be running a much bigger risk — being seen as a snitch by every officer in the station. Bang goes any possibility of winning the trust of my colleagues and getting any more inside stories of the workings of the police. Goodbye to patrolling the streets; hello to an office the size of a postage stamp and an endless rota diet of supervising the custody cells. I sacrificed a year and a half of my life to get here, to have an opportunity to see how the system works. And though it might sound paradoxical, the very reason I'm here is to report on this kind of abuse.

And so, I convince myself to do something amoral, to protect my role as an insider. In time, I will get to tell the story of this SNAFU without omitting a detail. By keeping my cover, I'll be able to show a side of the police that we never see, not even when there's footage of the abuse. How do the cops get away with it? Do they just bury the complaint? And, if so, is it difficult, or is it with the tacit support of senior officers? What exactly happens?

By writing about this cock-up, I might be able to prevent a thousand others.

"So, what am I supposed to say?" I ask Mano.

"Just tell them what happened," he says, completely confident.

Though he puts no pressure on me, he's suggesting I go along with the incident report written yesterday. There is no need to say anything more.

"Don't sweat it, I didn't rough him up that badly," says Mano. "Yeah, okay, I gave him a couple of punches, but I could have done worse."

"Yes … we know how these things go," says Fanny.

A dark-haired female officer wearing a Rolling Stones T-shirt and a leather jacket appears outside the commissariat. She gives me a perfunctory kiss on both cheeks, and tells me she works for the SAIP — the service that deals with investigations into prisoners in custody.

"I'll be seeing you for your interview," she says with a relaxed smile. "Don't worry, it's just a formality."

Half an hour later, I find myself sitting in her office on the third floor of the commissariat. The interview lasts twenty-two minutes. I recount the story as written in the incident report. I blame the kid. That done, the officer asks questions.

"So, did any of the officers strike the suspect while he was in the lobby?"

"No."

"While you were in the vehicle, did Officer García at any time shout, 'Shut your mouth' or 'What did you say, you little fucker?'"

Yes.

"Did Officer García say that?"

"No."

"Let's move on. Did Monsieur Konaté use threatening language when speaking to Officer García?

Not at first, but later, yes.

"Yes. He said he wasn't a real man, he threatened to take him on, one on one. And he laughed at him and said he was piss-weak."

"At any point, did Monsieur Konaté say: 'You just wait, me and my mate from the Compans estate will get you'?"

No.

"Yes."

"Did Monsieur Konaté repeatedly called Officer García a bastard?"

"Yes."

Only after the officer insulted Konaté first.

"Did Monsieur Konaté attempt to kick the police vehicle?"

No, but Officer García beat him up.

"I don't remember."

"Do you have anything else you'd like to add?"

"No."

She prints out my statement. I read it through and then sign it.

"Look, if you could see the TAJ record on this kid ... Four long pages!"

TAJ stands for *Traitement des antécédentes judiciaires* — the record of a suspect's previous offences. Though he has only just turned sixteen, Konaté has cropped up in at least twenty different investigations.

"Really? At his age?"

"Like I said, a TAJ record that runs to four pages. And then there's his mother. When I phoned her earlier, she swore at me and claimed that we were the ones who assaulted her son. You get the picture ..."

33

By the time I set off down the rue d'Hautpoul, it's 10.30 pm. I'm heading home, alone with my conscience. My head feels like lead, and so do my legs. Providing a false statement to cover up for a cop was never on my agenda. I had expected there would be brawls, I had thought of how to protect myself in the event of danger, but covering up for an officer who went too far was something I didn't see coming.

It's too late to go for a drink, but I need to spill my guts. To clear my head. My thoughts are whirling in a loop. False statement. Konaté. Police cock-up. I turn into the avenue Jean-Jaurès; the métro station is only a couple of yards away. I toss my cigarette butt on the ground.

About ten of my friends know that I'm working undercover, but I try not to talk about it with them too often. I keep my stories for my evenings with La Merguez, a friend I met at journalism college.

But I don't have the patience to wait for our next drink together. So, tonight, I text the story to a friend on Messenger. In a few short lines, I tell her how I lied. She immediately texts back: "I'm really worried that you're getting in too deep in this thing. You have to have limits. Because right now you're covering up for, quote-unquote, minor cock-ups. But what happens if it's something serious, what will you do then?"

Another friend weighs in: "I'm really shocked you'd go as far as that, even though, yeah, I understand that it all happened really quickly. How do you admit to making a false statement without shooting yourself in the foot? Even if it sheds light on the abuse, if I were you, I'd be afraid of retaliations, but most of all, I'd feel ashamed."

I don't reply. Did I make a mistake? Did I have a choice? I risked blowing my cover with the other officers. As an undercover journalist, I made the right decision. As a cop, I did exactly what my colleagues expected of me. As an individual and a human being, it's a very different matter. How far am I prepared to go?

On Monday evening, I finally meet up with La Merguez. We have arranged to meet up at "le Gob", a bar near the Place d'Italie where we're regulars.

While I'm waiting for him to arrive, I listen to the people sitting at the other tables. There's a group of guys arguing about *World of Warcraft* — the bar is a hangout for geeks and gamers. Maybe they're right to spend as much time as possible in a virtual world. It's a form of escape like any other. I could do with spending a couple of nights immersed in role-playing games. It might do me good to confront a hydra in its lair, or to fly on a dragon's back. I'm thinking about this when my friend shows up, a roll-up cigarette dangling from the corner of his mouth.

"Hey, Sergeant! How are things?"

Since I went uncover, he finds it funny to give me these little nicknames, probably as a reaction to my name for him in the book — because he looks like a merguez sausage, tall and stringy with copper-coloured skin. Between his endless digs at me, I manage to tell him about my more recent adventures. And I tell him how it has been weighing on me for the past two days.

He sips his lager, heaves a sigh, and thinks.

"Look, the way I see it, when you do something like that, you've crossed a line. You need to be careful not to get caught up in this shit. It might not be so easy to get out of. If I'm honest, you're kind of freaking me out."

He orders another round. We've got another half an hour before we have to go our separate ways. Him, to change the baby's nappies; me, to get an early night.

• • •

In the commissariat where I'm stationed, you hear racist, homophobic, and sexist remarks every day. They're made by a handful of officers, but they're tolerated or ignored by the others.

138

I've been undercover now for three months, and I've seen fellow officers slam a Black immigrant into a bus shelter and then throw him into the police van; rough up a Moroccan immigrant; assault young Konaté; and slap a number of people in custody, all of them Black, Arab, or dark-skinned.

Reviewing my brief experience of the force, I've realised that a suspect does not get beaten simply because he's caught bang to rights. Take the two young white cadets we arrested and who were accused by officers of being black-bloc anarchists. They wound up at the station tarred with the label of cop-hating cops. But they were not assaulted. It is over simplistic to say that they were spared simply because they were white. On the other hand, it's clear that at the commissariat where I'm working, other suspects have been beaten for much less.

These observations, made while on the job in a particular commissariat, prompt the thorny question: am I dealing with a series of isolated cases, or does the French police force tolerate racist behaviour in its ranks? In other words, do police officers treat French citizens differently based on the colour of their skin?

In 2009, two sociologists studied how police officers carried out random ID checks. They conducted the experiment, which they called "Racial Profiling in Paris", in two separate locations where ID checks are common: the Gare du Nord train station and the area around Châtelet. They were attempting to probe "a reputation". "Historically, and still today, police officers in France have a reputation of interacting differently with foreigners and those of foreign origin," they wrote.

According, they classified people according to skin colour: "Caucasian — Black — Arabic/North African — Indian/Pakistani — Asian (other)". The researchers also included criteria that might lead to police stopping an individual, such as how they were dressed and whether they were carrying a bag or rucksack. They set out three categories of clothing: "formal" (suit and tie), "casual" (T-shirts, jeans), and "youth" (sportswear and clothing associated with hip-hop, reggae, or electronic music).

To provide a control sample for their research, they carefully assessed the demographic of the people at both locations, visually classifying some thirty-eight thousand individuals.

The results of their survey showed there were a number of disparities between the demographic of those targeted by police officers and the overall demographics of those present:

Gender: men are between 3.5 times and 10 times more liked to be stopped than women. Young people are also more likely to be targeted. For example, on the square named the Fontaine des Innocents near Châtelet, young people made up only 50 per cent of those present, but fully 99 per cent of those subjected to police checks. Clothing is also a key factor: the effect of wearing youth clothing is "literally off the charts" and means an individual is between 5.7 and 16.1 times more likely to be stopped by officers. Lastly, "there is also a clear disparity when it comes to ethnic minorities".

More specifically:

Black people [are] 3.3 to 11.5 times more likely to be subjected to police checks than white people compared to their numbers within the population as a whole; for those of Arabic and North African origin, the figure is between 1.8 and 14.8 times greater.

According to the researchers, these disparities are significantly higher than those noted in comparable studies in Great Britain and the United States. "So we are faced with the fact that police officers disproportionately target individuals who are male, who wear youthful clothing, and those from ethnic minorities."

Slim Ben Achour, a lawyer at the Paris Court of Appeal and co-chair of "Discrimination", a commission within the Syndicat des Avocats de France (French Lawyer's Union), spent almost five years working to get the French police to admit to racial profiling. In 2015, he succeeded in having the government condemned for gross negligence. In their 2016 decision, the highest court of appeal in France, the Cour de Cassation, found the state culpable in three cases, and stated that "a police identity check carried out based on physical characteristics associated with real or supposed ethnic origin, without objective justification, is discriminatory".

In an interview, Slim Ben Achour relates how, throughout the five years he was fighting this legal battle, the government's defence was to argue that equal rights and anti-discrimination legislation did not apply to police identity checks.[10]

The appeal court's condemnation of the government coincides with my personal experience: in general, the attitude of police officers varies according to the ethnicity of an individual — as though the police apply a "presumption of guilt" to a section of the population.

If we look closely at the record of police cock-ups, ethnicity and skin colour also play an important role. The first thing that is startling is the lack of available information. The government, despite championing statistics as a measure of success and failure, has conducted no detailed analyses of police "blunders".

In June 2018, for the first time, the General Inspectorate of the National Police (IGPN) allowed access to official figures. "In a democracy, it is hardly unusual that people would wish to know how many people have died during police interventions," the head of the IGPN, Marie-France Monéger-Guyomarc'h, said.

According to the IGPN figures, fourteen people died during routine police actions between July 2017 and May 2018. But the IGPN quickly went on to specify that this figure related to "regrettable incidents" and was not "a list of police blunders". Moreover, the names of the those who died and the circumstances of their deaths were not disclosed.

In January 2019, a piece in the CheckNews section of the newspaper *Libération* attempted to review the number and the natures of these deaths.[11] That section of the newspaper takes the form of a question from a reader, which it attempts to clarify.

In this case, CheckNews was attempting to corroborate an article published by Mediapart in which Laurent Theron, 49, who was injured by a police flash-ball grenade during protests against changes to labour regulations in Paris in September 2016, described "Police crimes" as "racist". He went on to say: "Of the twenty to thirty people who die [in police custody] each year, 80 per cent are Black or Arabic, despite the fact that they represent only 10 per cent of the population."

The website Bastamag, described as "the most comprehensive database" on the subject of deaths in custody, reports that twenty to thirty people die at the hands of police officers each year (this includes operations by gendarmes and off-duty officers — as when a police officer kills someone with a service weapon while off duty). Bastamag offers no breakdown of these figures by ethnicity. However, the co-founder of the site, Ivan du Roy, told *Libération*:

> A simple glance, and the first names and surnames of those who died make it clear that immigrants and those from an immigrant background are hugely over-represented. That is a simple fact. But it is not enough to infer precise statistics. For this, we would need to know the skin colour of each victim, something that cannot directly be inferred from their name, and something that would be difficult to ascertain for incidents that occurred many years ago. It should be mentioned that this would also raise legal questions, since we are not permitted to gather statistics based on ethnicity.

These findings are corroborated by ACAT (Christian Action for the Abolition of Torture), which in 2016 published a report titled "On the Use of Force by the Police Nationale and the Gendarmerie". In its report, ACAT limits its analysis to those incidents in which "force was directly exerted by police and gendarmes", and thus reports only twenty-six deaths between 2005 and 2015. There is, however, a crucial detail in the report: of the twenty-six deaths, "at least twenty-two of these individuals were from ethnic minorities".

Therefore, even by the most conservative estimate, 85 per cent of deaths that result from situations involving gendarmes and/or officers of the Police Nationale are individuals from ethnic minorities (though it is impossible to judge how many of these were the result of police blunders).

The Larousse dictionary offers two definitions of the word "racism": first as "an ideology founded on the belief that there exists a hierarchy between human groups, of 'races'"; second — and this definition is less widely known in France — as "behaviour motivated by this ideology" such as "systematic hostility towards a specific category of individuals: e.g. anti-youth racism".

What can be done about systemic racist behaviour from law-enforcement officers?

When confronted with the same problem, Norway completely overhauled its training programme for police officers. Norwegian police officers are required to have three years' training (compared to twelve months for regular officers in France, and three months for an ADS like me), of which two full weeks are devoted to the subject of race and ethnicity.

The problem in France remains that, before we can

consider solutions, we must first acknowledge that the problem exists.

In May 2020, following the death in Minneapolis of George Floyd — a forty-six-year-old African American who died when a white policeman, Derek Chauvin, knelt on his neck for approximately eight to nine minutes — riots erupted across the United States, and there were #BlackLivesMatter protests around the world. In France, on 2 June 2020, twenty thousand people gathered outside the Tribunal de Paris in support of a committee called "Truth for Adama".

Adama Traoré was a young Black French citizen who died on his twenty-fourth birthday, 19 July 2016, during an arrest carried out by three gendarmes. In the absence of video footage of the incident, or any witnesses beyond the three gendarmes involved, a series of autopsies was conducted to determine whether or not Traore's death was caused by "positional asphyxia".

Following these protests in summer 2020, investigations by Mediapart, Arte radio, and StreetPress uncovered numerous discriminatory and racist comments made by serving police officers on social networks such Facebook and on private messaging services such as WhatsApp. Faced with mounting anger, the president, Emmanuel Macron, requested that Prime Minister Édouard Philippe and the minister for the interior, Christophe Castaner, urgently submit proposals to "improve the police professional code of ethics".

The point was further emphasised on 8 June 2020, when Jacques Toubon published the annual report of the *Défenseur des droits* — the Defender of Rights: complaints against the use of force by police had surged by 29 per cent in 2019.[12] Toubon stated that public confidence in the police and the gendarmerie was crucial to their effective functioning, and this in turn was founded on their respect for a professional code of ethics.

The findings of Toubon's report are incontestable:

> Since being appointed to the role [in 2014], the *Défenseur des droits* has requested that disciplinary proceedings be taken in thirty-six separate cases. However, despite the fact that such requests by the DDD have been rare compared to the number of cases reviewed over the period, not one has been acted upon.

On the day that Toubon's report was published, Castaner held a press conference on police brutality and racism. This marked a turning point for a minister who, until that point, had vigorously defended the police. "In recent weeks, too many have failed in their duty to the Republic. There have been revelations of racist remarks and discrimination. This is unacceptable," he said.

There followed a list of proposals intended to

"improve the professional code of ethics in law-enforcement agencies". The minister announced that the method of police restraint known as a "chokehold" would henceforth be prohibited, and proposed a "root-and-branch reform of the inspections made by the Ministry of the Interior" — through the IGPN, and the IGGN and IGA, the corresponding inspectorates for the gendarmerie — to allow them "greater independence in their dealing with law-enforcement agencies".

The minister concluded by saying: "There is no evidence of institutional racism or targeted violence."

On 17 June 2020, the newspaper *Le 1* published an investigative report, "Being Black in France", and, as part of it, a long article headlined "I Can't Breathe", written by Raoul Peck, the Haitian director of the documentary *I Am Not Your Negro*. In it, he stated that France was "in denial". "'Low-level' racism is still racism. It is just as hurtful ... The French would like to believe that racism exists only in the United States."

Peck went on to recount "an incident with the police" told to him by one of his daughter's friends.

With all the wisdom of a fourteen-year-old show-off, this boy tells me how he was held at a police station while an officer played Russian roulette, pointed his gun at the kid's head. He's laughing as he tells me this story. But I can see in his eyes that the incident has left its mark. Needless to say, the officer didn't see him as a child; at best, he saw him as a "delinquent".

This was precisely the same way that Mano saw Konaté as a "chouf", a dealer's look-out boy, and not simply as a teenage boy playing the tough guy and listening to rap. This approach dehumanises the victim, and leads to a presumption of guilt. Unconsciously, the officers at my commissariat believe that the sort of person they refer to as a "bastard" doesn't deserve to be treated with "fairness" or "impartiality"; in short, he doesn't deserve their respect. Not because of what he has done, but because of who he is.

Once individuals are dehumanised, anything can be justified, including beating up a juvenile or an immigrant. And I have to say that, in the instances of police brutality that I witnessed, there were no repercussions whatsoever.

34

One morning, the cops show up at my apartment to pick me up. I am still sprawled in my bed on the mezzanine, stark naked. They knock on the door. I quickly pull on a pair of boxers and a T-shirt, and go to open the door, my eyes still thick with sleep.

It all goes peacefully. The moment I saee them in the doorway, I know what is happening. This is the end of my little game, my undercover operation.

I don't remember any of their faces — which is strange, because faces are usually the first thing I commit to memory. I follow them without a word: handcuffs, police van, custody cell.

They take me to a place I don't recognise. It's certainly not a police station, or one of the offices of the Police Judiciaire. The whole place is bubble-gum pink — the floors, the ceilings, even the carpeted walls. What branch of the police service looks like this?!

I spend a minute pacing in circles in this bizarre room equipped only with a table and a window with opaque glass.

Two officers appear; they have come to question me. They settle themselves on the folding chairs they've brought. They look like twins with identical hair, parted on the left and combed over to hide premature bald patches. The Tweedledee and Tweedledum of the intelligence services. They politely offer me a coffee, which I accept.

"So, you're a journalist," says the first cop, visibly annoyed.

"Yes, I am."

"This is going to cost you dearly; you know that …"

"Has my lawyer arrived?"

"Not yet."

Inside the interrogation room an alarm goes off, a shrill wail that wakes me from this nightmare. I grab the phone under my pillow. I open my eyes. It's 4.25 am. My undercover mission has started infecting my dreams.

35

Ludo: Do we have someone called Guillaume in the station?

Vargo: Yeah, he's an officer with the J2.

Ludo: He just topped himself …

Xavier: Is that definite? Where did you hear that?

Vargo: Yeah, it's definite.

Ludo: A friend just told me.

Xavier: Fuck.

Another officer: He was doing an internship with the GSQ.[13]

Xavier: Was he working from home or out of the Commissariat Principal?[14]

Benjamin: Shit …

Vargo: He wasn't working out of the CP …

Xavier: OK.

Vargo: His name's Guillaume Ariège.

Xavier: I know the name, I just can't put a face to it.

Vargo posts a photo of the officer who has just committed suicide. He is wearing a black suit and tie.

Xavier: Oh, shit, I do know him...
Loïc: Fuck, he's got the locker next to mine. I was chatting to him yesterday.
Ludo: Serious shit :-/
Bullitt: Yeah. A fucking tragedy.

Vargo posts four crying emojis.

Rodrigue: Shit.
Natacha: Shit. Anyone here know the guy well? Seemed like a good bloke. Not depressed or anything. Who confirmed this?
Benjamin: You can never tell. I mean, how many times have you told people you're fine when really you're not? And let's face it, we only get to chat to each other for like, five, ten minutes between shifts.
Natacha: True ... That's the worst bit. We don't really know what the people we're working with are thinking ... It's terrifying.
Benjamin: It's because weakness isn't tolerated in the force. So no one admits to it.
Natacha: It's so fucking dumb. I mean, we're all human beings. We've all got shit to deal with ... Times when we're down.
Benjamin: Yeah, but the thing is, we're cops.

36

The police force has one of the highest suicide rates of any profession. In 2017, fifty-one police officers took their own lives. In 2018, it was thirty-five officers. Our former colleague is the thirty-third officer to commit suicide in 2019. By the end of the year, the grisly toll will have risen to fifty-nine.

Sebastian Roché, the director of research at the CNRS — the National Centre for Scientific Research — has specialised in working with the police. In an interview published in *Le Monde* on 20 April 2019, he mentions the rate of "over-suicide" among police officers, and specifies:

> We've known for forty years that the suicide rate among police officers is significantly higher than among similar individuals in the general population, i.e. men aged between thirty-five and forty-five. In June 2018, a report published by the Senate indicated that the suicide rate in the police force was 36 per cent higher than the general population.[15]

To me, the thirty-third officer to commit suicide in 2019 is not an abstract number. He is someone who worked here at the commissariat. I study the photo again. He's a handsome guy with short, dark hair holding a brand-new mobile phone. He worked with the JS, a different brigade from mine. I don't think I ever ran into him in the corridors.

When I get to the rue Erik-Satie, I find Marvin, a rookie officer, hanging around outside the station. He didn't know the guy either.

"We don't know if it was a suicide or an accident. He was on leave, but he took his service weapon home with him. His colleagues from the J2 all showed up at the commissariat, but they're not working," Marvin tells me. Some were in tears; others were in shock. They hung out downstairs and chatted. Some officers take their service weapons home when they go on leave. Now, the Commissaire is in the shit because she's the one who signed the authorisation for him to take the weapon home with him.

After the terrorist attacks in Paris and Saint-Denis in November 2015, Jean-Marc Falcone, the director-general of the Police Nationale, in response to appeals from the police unions, approved a "temporary dispensation" allowing officers to take their Sig Sauer pistols home with them.

In January 2016, Bernard Cazeneuve, the then minister of the interior, signed an order extending the temporary dispensation to any state of emergency. Since then, whenever a state of emergency is declared, "any off-duty police officer may carry his service weapon for the duration of that state of emergency, including in areas outside the territorial jurisdiction where he works".

Eventually, what had been an exceptional arrangement became standard procedure. In June 2016, an Islamic terrorist killed two police officers in their home in Magnanville. It was this tragedy that prompted President François Hollande's government to extend the dispensation outside states of emergency.

Instructions issued by the Ministry of the Interior detail the three conditions under which officers may carry their weapons when off duty: they must declare the fact to the head of their service; they must have regularly taken part in firearms training over the previous year (three sessions of thirty cartridges), and they must have taken part in at least one firearms-training session in the previous four months.[16]

The measure has created a new normal: these days, an officer has access to their service weapon twenty-four hours a day. Which in turn prompts a thorny question: has a safety measure taken in the wake of terrorist attacks contributed to the high suicide rate among police officers?

In April 2019, the minister of the interior, Christophe Castaner, set up CAPS, a Suicide Prevention Alert Unit.

He did so, in his words, to "end the fear, end the shame, end the silence". Yet the minister opened his statement by saying: "The fact that police officers who wished to do so have been permitted carry their service weapon between their home and their place of work has had no impact on the increased rate of suicide using service weapons."

The minister's argument is cynical, to say the least. If the rate of "suicide by service weapon" has not increased dramatically since this measure, it is for one simple reason: it has already reached a high point.

The sociologist Nicolas Bourgoin had already offered a statistical analysis in his 1997 report "Suicide rates in the Police Nationale".[17] In the French population at large, men between the ages of twenty-five and fifty-four commonly commit suicide by hanging. Among police officers, in 75.6 per cent of cases, they use their service revolver.

This figure underscores a vital fact: while the service weapon might not be the *cause* of the high rates of suicide in the force, it is certainly the *means*. Bourgoin speaks of "easy access to the radical solution represented by the service revolver".

He lists the salient factors that explain the high suicide rate among police officers: "access to firearms"; "alcohol abuse"; "work schedules deleterious to family life" (a high divorce rate); "public indifference or even antipathy"; and "a legal system that can be a source of

Valentin Gendrot

frustration and confusion" (police officers have to live with many court decisions they consider unjust). In an interview with *Les Jours*, Noémie Angel, the head of CAPS, adds that "the post-traumatic stress disorder resulting from constant exposure to scenes of violence" and "being constantly faced with death" further increases the risk of suicide. One of the objectives of CAPS, she says, is to "remove the stigma from asking for help" from a doctor or a psychologist.[18]

• • •

On our WhatsApp group, Steph, the Brigadier-Chef, is looking for volunteers to deputise for members of the J2 on Friday afternoon: their shift clashes with the funeral of their fellow officer. I volunteer. Out in the hallway, I run into Mano.

"Did you sign up for the shift on Friday?" I ask.

"No, I'm not doing it for something like that. I mean, look, we don't know the whole story, but we don't want officers to end up looking like losers. Anyway, it's on a voluntary basis. I would be really pissed off if they ordered us to work the shift."

"Yeah, but surely it's important for his fellow officers to be able to pay their last respects?"

Mano sighs; he seems unconvinced. In the end, the powers decide to spare me working on Friday. ADS overtime costs the administration too much, I am told.

• • •

A few days later, all the officers in the brigade are summoned to the incident room. A Commandant addresses the assembled group.

"I'd like to thank you all for coming to work last Friday, following the tragic death of a fellow officer. Thanks to you, twenty officers were able to attend the funeral. Some wore full-dress uniform. It looked really class. We were able to parade before and after the funeral."

He repeats this expression several times: "It looked really class."

"As for our fellow officer, there is no way of knowing whether he did what he did for professional or personal reasons," the Commandant continues. "He seemed in good form. We can only wait for the conclusions of the investigation, though it's possible we'll never really know what happened. Thanks again to all of you."

The Commandant leaves the incident room. The daily grind carries on as normal. Down in the changing room, the dead officer's old locker stands empty. A note has been taped to the metal door. "As a mark of respect to our late colleague and friend, please do not put anything in this locker. Thank you."

"That's all well and good," says Tacos, "but at some point, we'll have to move on."

37

Some cop who works in my brigade posts a link to an article in *Le Parisien*. "Hurricane Miguel: man gravely injured by falling lamppost in Paris."

The cop: Let's hope he was a dealer. (LMAO emoji)
Bullitt: LOL
Another officer: Or a hipster.

38

This morning, Stan does his usual number. As roll-call is read out, he heaves a sigh. He doesn't like the people he's being sent out on patrol with. As far as he's concerned, they're bad cops, incompetents.

"So, who's driving?" he asks.

I tell him it's me. His eyes widen, and he sighs again. Stan wants the officers in his squad to be like him: fearless hunters chasing down bastards.

His view of the force includes a category he calls "losers", and I am one of them. I'm a four-eyed ADS with fuck-all experience, a guy who tails behind and never takes the initiative.

He doesn't seem to realise that I'm doing my level best to fit in. For example, I've just bought Natacha's old "tactical vest". I paid thirty euros for a sleeveless multi-pocket jacket with polyethylene plates designed to protect the abdomen and the thorax. All my colleagues wear them on patrol. On the back, I've stuck a large rectangular, reflective police badge.

I've also downloaded "Actu 17" — an app that

collates minor crime stories used by most of the officers in the station. I could also do with getting a better flashlight than the station-issue Maglite. Often they're missing, and half of them don't work. I'd like to buy a better pair of gloves, but I'd have to pay for all this gear. My colleagues pay for their gear out of their own pockets.

Roll-call ends.

"Do you want to drive, or do want me to take over?" Stan asks as we're filing out of the incident room. He clearly doesn't want me behind the wheel, despite the fact that I've been selected.

"Whatever you want," I say irritably.

As I walk down the corridors behind Stan, I feel as though I'm stalking a celebrity. Other officers come over to talk to him, shake his hand. Stan is a princeling; he has his own little court. When we get down to the garage, Stan climbs behind the wheel of the Peugeot 208.

39

"Hey, that guy over there! He's doing a runner!"

About a hundred yards away, a guy breaks into a run. We first spotted him fifteen minutes earlier as he slunk away just before we could check his papers. Loïc and I race through the streets after him.

At first, I find myself trailing Loïc. It's the first time I've had to chase someone. In police jargon, we call it a "fixture". It's not easy to sprint wearing heavy Ranger boots and a cumbersome tactical vest. I need to be careful not to drop my radio and wind up looking like a moron.

Stan takes the radio and announces the race.

"Runner, Porte d'Aubervilliers. Male suspect wearing black, carrying a blue rucksack."

I quickly overtake Loïc. I'm determined to prove to him, to myself, to Stan, that I'm not a loser.

The suspect races across the roundabout at Porte de la Villette, weaving between cars, heading towards Aubervilliers. That's outside our jurisdiction, but fuck it. I keep running, into the roundabout, zigzagging between cars. The guy doing a runner might have something on him — some weed or coke stashed in his bag — or he might just need to get the fuck out of here. Or maybe he's just scared of cops.

If I catch the guy, I'll be a made man. I'll have taken a suspect single-handed and earned the respect of the whole brigade. "Gendrot? He's a decent cop," they'll say. I don't know why I feel I need to win their approval. After all, I shouldn't care. I'm here to write a no-holds-barred report on life in the force, not to win their admiration. But that is part of it.

You could say I've been taken over by "swot syndrome". I'm so desperate to fit in, to focus on doing what they do, that I've internalised their codes. It's something I've experienced in other undercover missions. Most of the time, you're not pretending to be a model employee — there's no acting involved, you simply become a model employee.

And, right now, the model employee inside my head is telling me I have to catch this stranger running away. Regardless of why he's running.

But I still need to arrest him. Assuming I catch up, how do I stop him? I picture myself tackling the guy, like a defender on a football pitch. But I might hurt him …

I find myself alone on the boulevard. I've lost sight of the suspect. *Where did he go? Shit!* I'm panting for breath.

"He ducked into the market," a passer-by tells me.

Behind the wheel of the Peugeot, Stan is caught in a traffic jam and shows up too late. As does Loïc. We huddle together. Another patrol shows up, and then another. The guy is nowhere to be found. Where the fuck did he go?

Stan insists we keep searching. We search the neighbouring streets before coming back to where we started. Nothing: not a sign. I sit in the back of the car, pouring with sweat. Stan is furious: "For fuck's sake, he wasn't even running that fast!"

40

In our WhatsApp group, Rodrigue posts a screenshot of a webpage called the "Register of Shame", an up-to-date list of the annual suicides in the military and the forces of law and order. There have been nine in the gendarmerie. Two in the prison service. Three in the army. Seven in the local police force. One in the transport police force. None among customs officers. Forty-three in the Police Nationale. A total of sixty-five. Last year, this final toll was eighty-eight deaths.

One of the officers in the group says: "This is not right. We need to organise some barbecues."

A month earlier, on 30 May 2019, France Info radio reported that the director of the Police Nationale, Eric Morvan, had sent a memorandum calling on senior officers to "take action" about the suicide rate. Morvan called for greater recognition for officers, for a more approachable atmosphere, for more "social interaction" within the force.

It was suggested that senior officers look into the

way in which decorations were awarded, to ensure this was done in a "ceremonial context" rather than as an "impersonal transaction". He mentioned a pre-existing internal social network nicknamed "Radio Police", intended to allow officers to discuss things frankly and openly. The memorandum also recommended that the police force organise social gatherings like "barbecue, sports events, or picnics".

For my fellow officers, the "barbecue memorandum" was a symbol of the yawning gap between the senior officers and the rank and file. Sebastian Roché comes to the same conclusion: "There is insufficient public policy dealing with the specific challenges of the role of police officer. And the greatest threat to the police force is not criminals, it is suicides."

41

By the time I'm four months into my undercover mission, I've slipped into a monotonous routine. I know that during each four-day "cycle" I'll be expected to do two days on sentry duty outside the commissariat, one or two days supervising custody cells, and only one day out on the streets, on patrol.

Today, I'm posted outside. It's often the same familiar faces, ADSs, rookie cops like Ludo or Marvin. I get along okay with them. We chat, we laugh. I've finally been accepted. The other officers consider me one of their own. I've played football with them a couple of times — my one opportunity to shine, certainly more so than I do out on the streets. I might not be the best cop in the nineteenth arrondissement, but at least I laugh at their jokes.

Because, deep down, I'm not so different to them. They remind me of where I'm from. Most, like me, are from the provinces. Most, like me, come from working-class or middle-class families. I don't have to try too hard to fit in. They're like the friends I had in primary and secondary school, the guys I play football with, the kind of people I've been hanging round with since I was a kid.

This touches a sore spot in me, a feeling I have never resolved. The sense that, no matter where I am, I never truly belong. Too posh for the world I grew up in, too uncouth for the world of Paris journalism.

Wherever I find myself, my instinctive approach is always the same: don't say too much. And at the commissariat, I stay out of the factional rivalries between Stan and his "hunters" on the one hand, and their antithesis, led by Toto, on the other. Being tight-lipped and tactful has its advantages: it means that I can hang out with either group.

Not much happens during sentry duty outside the commissariat, but it's an ideal place to watch and listen.

"I was with the girl the other night," Ludo is telling some cop I don't recognise. "It was fucking amazing. She gave me a blowjob, I shot my wad, and then got the hell out of there, fast! Puts a spring in your step, I tell you!"

The other cop walks off with a smile on his face. This bragging about sexual conquests — real or imagined — is routine, one of the most clichéd tropes of male bonding. I sometimes indulge in it so as not to stand out from the crowd, although ordinarily it is something I wouldn't talk about even with close friends. One night, as I'm going off shift, I mention to my colleagues that I'm hooking up with a girl. The next morning, some cop slaps me on the back and says, "How's it going, big boy? Did you give it to her good last night?"

Right now, it's just me and Ludo. He quickly starts telling me about his childhood.

"Back in secondary school, I was a loser. I was a puny little runt with acne. I hung out with a lot of dodgy people."

Rather than sit the baccalaureate exam, Ludo took a vocation qualification in telecommunications and, like his father and brother before him, joined the army. He dreamed of being a paratrooper, but his eyesight was too poor, so he signed up for the infantry.

"I tell you, it was hell. I fucking hated it."

Ludo talks about the night marches through the forest, the rigid discipline.

"Compared to the army, the force is a walk in the park, believe me. Like, back in school, if you fucked up, there were teachers who'd let you off with a warning, three, four times. In the army, you make one mistake, and the whole unit gets punished. You quickly learn your lesson."

"The police academy was pretty strict too," I say.

"It's not the same, not even close."

Marvin and a couple of other officers come outside with their coffees, and stand around and chat. Toto comes out to join them, clearly riled. Stan and his squad have just made an arrest. They came across five teenagers who'd just stolen a pair of AirPods. Stan and his guys gave chase and caught two of them.

"He's a jammy bastard!" Toto says. "It's crazy how lucky he is!"

He and Marvin head back out on patrol, leaving me alone with Ludo. Yesterday, Ludo went to renew his "HK" certificate — his authorisation to use a submachine gun. He spent the whole morning from 8.15 to half past one proving his proficiency.

"One of the girls fired into the fucking ceiling … I mean, seriously, how is that even possible?"

I don't react; I know for me it would be quite possible.

Today, while on guard duty with me, Ludo's brawny fingers are gripping a submachine gun.

"So, what time does the terrorist get here?" he jokes. "He said he was going to drop by."

"Maybe he's running late. Have you got his number?"

"Yeah. I really have an urge to shoot things up!"

As a joke, Ludo aims his submachine gun at a worker on a building site, a passer-by, and then a pigeon.

"Oh, by the way, I should say, if anyone complains, there's a round in the chamber, but I put the safety on."

A submachine gun has a curved magazine that holds thirty rounds, and a four-position selective-fire trigger: safety, cocked, two-round burst, and fully automatic fire.

"I've got another clip in my pocket," Ludo says.

"Cool," I say, just for something to say.

"I know it's against the rules, I know we're not supposed to chamber a round, but I think that's dumb. The chief police — well, the ex-chief — didn't want us chambering a round in case of accidents. Apparently, the new chief is all in favour, but he hasn't officially announced it yet.

• • •

By the end of the day, Ludo's wrist is aching. Carrying a submachine gun is exhausting. It doesn't look like the terrorist is planning to show up today. Only a succession of people come in to file complaints, or to report the loss of official documents — ID cards, passports, residents permits.

We're bored stiff. The heat is stifling; there is no one coming to the commissariat. Under my bulletproof vest, I'm pouring with sweat. Suddenly, the radio crackles.

"Incoming projectiles!" comes the voice of a cop with the BSG.

Suddenly, there is panic at the station. But I'm still posted outside the front door, feeling frustrated.

Toto climbs into a squad car, flicks on the lights and sirens, and drives off in a squeal of rubber. I hear what happens next over the radio, like listening to a football match.

"Mind your heads, guys, they're tossing frozen

onions out of the windows," says an excitable officer.

It sounds like a forceful police intervention. There are screams from the radio.

A little while later, a squad car drops off two BSG officers who are restraining the young man they arrested. Another car shows up with the young man's moped in the back.

A couple of minutes later, Toto reappears. He ambles up to us and growls.

"Thing is, they didn't even catch the right guy, actually. It was a complete cock-up."

42

Stan's best mate at the commissariat is Charles, known to everyone as Charly. They were at the police academy together. Charly's locker is next to mine, so before roll-call we sometimes chat. He's funny, friendly, and built like a barn with a bull neck that makes him look like a rugby prop-forward.

"I've been doing this job for seven years, and I'm still amazed by the sheer stupidity of human beings. Here in the nineteenth, I thought I'd seen everything, but apparently not. When I tell my mother stories about what goes on, she says, 'You're making it up.' I wish! So, what have they got you doing today, big guy?"

"Custody supervision."

"In that case, we're working together."

I'm ready before he is, so I head off to get us a couple of coffees before going on shift. We get along pretty well, me and Charly.

It's 6.02 am. when I get to the bench and relieve the nightshift while I wait for Charly.

"There's eleven in custody," says the cell supervisor.

"Three brothers: one had more than three hundred euros on him, and we put the money in the safe. The other two had about a hundred euros each. They're pretty chilled. And then, there are four adult prisoners."

"Okay."

"Then there's a drunk arsehole."

"Okay. What about him, the one sitting on the bench?"

"He's another arsehole. He was supposed to be sent for a psych evaluation at five o'clock yesterday, but no one knew who was supposed to take him. So, he's still there. He bit an officer yesterday, pissed on the floor during the night. And every now and then, he starts screaming — but you'll see that for yourself."

I get freaked out by unstable prisoners. What if they go batshit crazy?

The cells are only half full. With only eleven people in custody, there won't be much to do, so it's a good day to chat. Charly settles himself behind the bench, fills out a few forms, and then answers my questions.

"I was an ADS for four and a half years. In the beginning, I was a traffic cop, but then, after I injured my knee, I worked in the twentieth arrondissement as a cell supervisor. I did that for eight or nine months. I tell you, we smashed a few faces, man!"

He reels off a long list of cases where guys got a punch in the face for the slightest misstep. He remembers seeing a guy covered in blood from a beating, while he went in to mop up the evidence.

"Tell you what, if my boss opened a cell door and saw a guy with his face bashed in, she'd just say, 'Ah … Maybe I'll come back a little later!'"

Charly's stories make my blood run cold; I'm finding it difficult to seem offhand. The constant violence of the daily grind is starting to take its toll on me. What I find astonishing, aside from the violent incidents, is that the officers feel as though they're untouchable. As though there's no chain of command, no supervision by senior officers. As though, based on nothing more than a mood or a whim, an officer can choose to be violent or not.

"One year, we racked up six thousand prisoners in custody, and we probably beat the shit out of half of them."

I start to wonder whether he's lying. I'm a little dubious. Three thousand guys beaten up in the space of a year would mean an average of seven or eight a day. Instinctively, I launch the Actu 17 app.

"Hey, we've just arrested a bunch of guys who beat up officers outside a nightclub," I tell Charly.

"Any injuries?"

"Yeah, a broken ankle and a couple of days off work."

"They shouldn't have bothered arresting them. They should have stuffed them in the boot of the squad car," says Charly.

Other headlines on Actu 17 include a lot of incidents that send my stress levels soaring. "Five years for driver who ran down gendarme"; "Teenage girl stripped and raped in city basement". It's enough to make anyone paranoid.

Charly recommends a book.

"I don't know if you've heard of it. It's called *Fear Has Switched Sides*, by some journalist, Ploquant or Ploquin, I can't remember.[19] Read it, you'll see — what he describes is exactly what we're going through right now."

I know the book he's talking about; I've heard the author being interviewed. In it, Frédéric Ploquin talks to police officers who explain that these days they feel they've been abandoned, that they've become targets. "Every day, every night, police officers start their shifts with a knot of fear in their bellies. Faced with crooks and thugs of all shapes and sizes, the police no longer measure up," he writes.

Towards the end of the shift, a group of teenagers is brought into custody. I recognise a boy who was here only a week ago. I go to talk to him.

"Capron?"

"What?" mutters the lanky teenager sprawled on the mattress.

He's got one of those trendy haircuts that's shaved at the sides but is long and curly on top.

"Still here, I see ..." I flash him a smile. "Seems like you can't stay out of trouble, kid."

He gets to his feet and briefly explains why he's here. A week ago, he was referred to court and got off with a slap on the wrist. Today, he and the others have been arrested for a gang mugging during which they stole a tablet and an MP3 player.

"I didn't do nothing this time," he says defensively.

"You're really determined to fuck up your life."

A couple of months ago, I would never have said such a thing. I hardly recognise myself. I may not be slapping prisoners, but I have the strange feeling that I'm starting to become a cop just like my colleagues: hardened and disillusioned.

43

There's another flurry of messages on the WhatsApp group.

> **Bullitt**: Another cop committed suicide in Toulouse. Hanged himself.
> **Natacha**: Jesus, that's even worse.
> **Benjamin**: Worse I'm not sure it's worse.
> **Bullitt**: He'd been without pay for 24 months after a disciplinary hearing.

On Thursday 20 June 2019, a forty-five-year-old police officer took his life. He killed himself in his own home. "The whole union feels immense grief and sadness. Sébastien was the father of three children, our thoughts and prayers are with them, and with his partner, his family, his relatives, and his fellow officers," reads a post on the Facebook page of the Unité SGP Police-Force Ouvrière.

Two days earlier, the officer had appeared before a disciplinary tribunal for "improper financial dealings", accused of paying a bribe in order to secure a transfer.

What kind of situation had the officer found himself in? Was he looking for a favour, or simply a means of escape? The press release provides no further information. Is there any other poorly paid profession where an individual would be willing to pay a bribe to get a transfer?

Tacos: It's a massacre.

Farid: Unbelievable.

Natacha: It's not really surprising that the guy completely snapped … There's nothing worse than financial problems. This government is a shower of complete bastards. They're heartless.

Ludo: Hey, wait up, you don't even know why he was suspended …

Natacha: Who gives a shit? Either you fire someone and they've got some chance of finding another a job. Or you suspend them on full pay, or allow them to work on the side. But you can't do that when you're suspended without pay, you've got no salary, and you're not allowed to work elsewhere because you're still a public servant.

44

On 27 June 2018, the French Senate publishes a report titled "Overcoming Discontent Within Law Enforcement: an imperative for the Republic". After the usual sad platitudes — "the parlous state of morale among police officers" — the elected members of the Senate focus on the "commonplace problems" of police officers serving in the area of Île-de-France.

In its report, the senatorial commission notes that "cases where as many as five police officers in Paris are forced to share a 20-square-metre apartment, alternately occupied by those taking day shifts and night shifts, with some even sleeping in their cars, are not uncommon".

The report also lists "a range of problems linked to the nature of the profession": "being regularly confronted by death"; "irregular work patterns"; "straitened financial circumstances"; "geographical postings that are imposed rather than voluntary"; "greater operational responsibilities" ("driven by a number of concurrent threats — an increase in terrorist activity, unprecedented pressures in migration, widespread social protests"); and the "the steadily mounting threat of violence towards them". The senators conclude their dismal survey with "the permanent uncertainty of roles and procedures".

The management of the Police Nationale is also skewered: "too distanced from work in the field and unresponsive to the day-to-day realities and problems faced by officers of officers, [the administration] has demotivated officers and contributed to a poorer work ethic". Relations between the police, the media, and the general population are described as "sources of significant problems"; the connection between the police force and the justice system is diplomatically described as "clearly crumbling".

The title, noting a "malaise" within the police force, suddenly sounds like a tepid euphemism for much deeper problems.

Back when I was working at the psychiatric hospital, I remember an ADS who (illegally) took a second job as a security guard at Parc des Princes stadium in order to make ends meet. I remember the self-mocking comment of Jérémy, who worked with me at I3P: "The police are delinquents who took the right turning."

In 2019, the year I spent undercover in the commissariat, a movie directed by Ladj Ly called *Les Misérables* was a huge success, with over two million tickets sold at the French box office. The film is set in a troubled working-class estate in the suburbs of Clichy-Montfermeil in Île-de-France. A squad attached to the BAC makes a catastrophic cock-up. The whole scene was caught on film by a drone; the police spend most of the movie doing everything they can to recover the video and hush up the incident — and they succeed. In this hyper-realistic film (which won the Jury Prize at the Cannes Film Festival), the social status of those who live on the estate is contrasted with those of the three cops in the main roles.

In an interview with *Elle*, the director was questioned on this point: "In *Les Misérables*, we realise that the police are no better off than the people they're policing," Ladj Ly says bluntly. "When you look into what their lives are like [the police], you realise it's a tragedy. They live in low-rent housing, they have shitty salaries, they're permanently depressed. In the end, you realise that our lives in the cities are better than theirs."

"Tragedy." Precisely the word Bullitt used after the officer at our station committed suicide.

Imagine a job where everything around you is falling apart: the company cars, the premises, the equipment. To rub salt into the wound, you're forced to wear a uniform that instantly elicits hostility from many people. Your training is rushed and slapdash, you are forced to deal with volatile situations, and — to add insult to injury — you are expected to reach often ridiculous quotas, "to rack up the numbers".

You're already on thin ice when senior officers decide to put a little more weight on your shoulders: you must always look smart, and your behaviour must be exemplary. This is covered in the famous mnemonic drummed into us at the police academy, DIILER: "dignity, integrity, impartiality, loyalty, exemplary conduct, and, above all, respect for every individual".

Is it reasonable to hurriedly train law-enforcement officers, make them work in pitiful conditions, and then demand that they act as role models? No, obviously not. It's neither reasonable nor workable.

During my time undercover, one thing became patently clear. In theory, cops are supposed to fight the violence, the racism, and the sexism in our society. In practice, they are often in the vanguard when it comes to such vices. We can discuss the reasons why this is so, but the fact remains. That's how things work in a commissariat. It is like a football changing room — an atmosphere of toxic masculinity where violent individuals are tolerated and rarely challenged. Because you have to make do with the people you have. With the resources you've been allocated.

So when cops fuck up, everyone sticks together, and more often than not, senior officers sweep what they like to think of as "mistakes" under the carpet. In most cases, they have little choice; since they demand the impossible of the men and women on the streets, the least they can do is cover for them.

45

I'm out on patrol with the Major again. When I'm with his crew, I have two options: I can drive, or I can sit in the back seat, as I'm doing this morning. Having to drag yourself out of bed at 4.25 am to issue some fines is a pain in the arse. It is 7.10 am. At the wheel of the Renault Mégane, Karine is driving slowly, since her car has no rear-view mirror. The windshield is still cracked from a speed bump taken a little too quickly. We've been waiting for it to be replaced for the past three weeks.

"TN19 to TVTJ."

"TVTJ receiving," says the Major.

"Scheduled security operation at the Passerelle du Millénaire footbridge at 07:30 hours".

"Understood."

The preposterous missions allocated to the police. The orders come from above, and there's no way to avoid them. Don't even think of challenging them or questioning them: to think is to disobey. Being an ADS, I get a lot of callouts like this. A week ago, Toto and I spent Saturday morning patrolling the Gare Rosa-

Parks. There was not a soul on the streets around the train station. It was completely futile. Earlier, we had been sent to patrol the market in Belleville. It was pouring rain, so there were no street hawkers flogging their wares. We sat in the car like idiots. On another occasion, an officer told me how he'd spent several hours watching garbage collectors picking up trash. It's tough to find meaning in your work 24/7.

Today, we're expected to secure a footbridge, a wooden pedestrian bridge used by a handful of passers-by. In theory, it's a surveillance op. Street fights and pickpockets are regularly reported here. In practice, at 7.30 am, the only people are commuters heading to work.

"Major, should I swing by the roundabout at La Villette to kill time?" Karine asks pointedly.

"Go ahead."

We drive. Around the roundabout, and then down the various major thoroughfares, cruising at 20, maybe 25kph along the rue Émile-Bollaert, the rue d'Aubervilliers, the boulevard McDonald. We all know we're heading nowhere. At 7.25, Karine puts the car into reverse. Rising up before us is the famous wooden footbridge. Next to it, a small, deserted park and an empty street. We stay in the car.

Through the misted windows, we watch the comings and goings of pedestrians. We're simply maintaining a police presence. It's called community policing. Reassuring the locals.

"Pretty quiet this morning," says the Major.

"Yeah, it's been quiet all week," say Karine.

"And what with it being Ramadan ..."

After five minutes' surveillance, there is no security operation. Jo, who is sitting on my right, is watching videos on his phone. I'm texting my friend La Merguez. 7.40 am. On the radio, Mylène Farmer is singing: "*Tu t'entêtes à te foutre de tout / Mais pourvu qu'elles soient douces / D'un poète tu n'as que la lune en tête / Des mes rondeurs tu es K.O.*"

We are still sitting waiting when George Michael takes over, singing "Wake Me Up Before You Go-Go". Over the police radio, we hear that the clutch on the police van has just gone. It had only just left the commissariat, and now needs to get back to the garage. PS Alpha squad are stuck on the steep hill on the rue de Belleville in a van that refuses to budge. It takes a whole organisation to round up the officers still at the station, send out a couple of crews to bring them back to the commissariat, and assign them to other squads. We still haven't moved — we're too busy on a security operation of the utmost importance.

It is 7.54 am.

"So, do we head off? asks Karine.

"No, let's wait for the hour," says the Major.

Another six minutes.

Karine stares into space. It puts me in a bad mood to stay here.

08:00 hours.

"Major to TN19," barks the Major.

"TN19 receiving."

"Safety operation completed. We are leaving the scene."

"Received and noted, thank you!"

Karine keys the ignition in the Mégane. We head off. To issue on-the-spot fines and deal with a homeless guy who's being kicked out of the lobby of an apartment building.

46

"Fucking Arab scum. You're not back in your country now, so learn some respect for women!"

In the hall lined with custody cells, Bullitt is roaring at a man who's just been brought in. He is suspected of raping a woman last night. The case is too high-profile for us to deal with — it will be handed over to the detectives of Police Judiciaire.

"If you don't calm down right now, you're gonna feel my fist in your fucking *blédard* face, you got that?

Bullitt is bellowing. He is staring the suspect right in the eye, his forehead practically pressed to the man handcuffed on his bench, who is looking pretty sheepish. I am surprised by how relaxed I feel watching this scene. I've grown accustomed to Bullitt's towering rages.

"Yeah, now there's a man who really knows how to respects women," mutters Stan as he passes by.

"PS Alpha, where are you?" shrieks Bullitt, my squad leader for the day. "Come on, shift your arses, get a fucking move on! And the girl … where's my little girlfriend?"

His "little girlfriend" is actually a female officer on the squad. Bullitt has a thing for her, so he makes off-colour remarks, "just banter", and calls her "my little girlfriend" all the time. He regularly comments on her appearance: "Look how pretty she is!" Standing facing him, his "girlfriend" simply smiles through gritted teeth. Bullitt somehow manages to frequently get assigned to go out on patrol with her. As he did today.

"Oh, there you are! You're looking fresh," says Bullitt with a snigger. "Hey, isn't she fresh, my little girlfriend?"

47

It's 2.40 pm, our shift is about to start. At the wheel, Toto starts up the van. In the passenger seat, Bullitt switches on the radio. A steady stream of American rap blares from the speakers, drowning out the belching engine noises of the heap of scrap that serves as our van.

While we're stopped at a red light, a feeble, dark-skinned man swamped by his baggy shirt and oversized trousers comes to the window to beg for money.

"Fuck off!" Bullitt yells at him. "Go on, get out of here!"

The man doesn't move. Bullitt gets out of the van. I follow. Bullitt grabs the man by the scruff of the neck and drags him back to the far side of the crash barrier.

"I don't want to see you out on the street, d'you hear me?"

The man does not move from where he was dumped.

We go back to driving aimlessly, waiting for our first callout.

"TN19 to PS Alpha."

"PS Alpha receiving," says Bullitt.

"Reports of a man threatening women with a stick outside of Belushi's, a youth hostel on the banks of the canal Saint-Denis. The caller describes him as an Indian immigrant wearing a white jacket and brown shoes, and has a blue backpack."

"PS Alpha responding."

We pull up outside Belushi's bar, near the rue de Crimée. The man who called in the complaint is waiting for us at the door.

"Well?" says Bullitt.

"That's the guy, over there."

We walk over to the man fitting the description. He is short, with dark hair, and is gripping a long wooden baton. Who knows where he found it? We surround him. The man doesn't seem particularly intimidated by our presence.

"Can I see your ID papers?" says Bullitt.

From his jacket pocket, the man takes out a phone and a folded sheet of paper.

"We've had reports of you attacking women? What d'you think you're doing?"

"I'm just touching their shoulders. It's a custom."

"A custom? Listen, you're not back in your country now. We don't do things like that here in France. And stop fidgeting. I said stop, or I'll stick one on you," says Bullitt threateningly.

"Go on. Hit me."

"Right, let's take him down to Porte de la Villette,"

Bullitt says loudly. "We're going to take you down to the Porte de la Villette, and if I see you hanging around here again, I'll toss you into the canal. Got it? If you set foot here again, I'll throw you into the canal d' Ourcq."

The man does not say a word, but lets us lead him away. We load him into the back of the van. When we reach Aubervilliers, we release him back into the wild. Basically, we simply relocate the problem, leaving the man to harass women outside our jurisdiction. Out of sight, out of mind.

We drive off.

"Come on, you little Uber shit, move it" Bullitt roars at a kid on a Deliveroo moped.

"Hey, Bullitt," says Tacos, "Let's stop the black Smart car that's just overtaken us. I spotted a couple of serious bastards inside."

The "serious bastards" are two Black men. We pursue the car. Bullitt signals for the driver of the vehicle to stop. He climbs out of the police van, gripping his LBD 40 gun, finger on the trigger, ready to fire. All this for a vehicle check.

The LBD 40 is a blast-ball launcher, originally intended to deal with extreme situations — such as threats with knives, or violent public disturbances — and was initially used only by specialists. From there, the use of blast balls spread to squads working in "problem" districts, and from there to any units dealing with violent offenders. Now, they're available to any cop with an authorisation.[20] Bullitt has one.

"Sir, could I see the documents relating to this vehicle?" Tacos asks the driver.

While he checks the documents, I keep an eye on the passenger. A little way off, Bullitt, still gripping his LBD 40, is waving on traffic.

"Go on, for fuck's sake, move it," he roars at a driver.

The papers for the Smart car are all in order. They drive off. We get back into the van.

I didn't say a word during the vehicle check. I feel like I'm riding with a gang that has unlimited powers.

48

"I'll have to ask you to come with us, Monsieur."

This is the first time I've worked with Max, and one of the few times I've heard a cop respectfully address someone as Monsieur. Over the past few weeks, I've found myself addressing everyone with the same casual French "*tu*", except old people.

Max respects the police code of ethics, which states that officers should address members of the public as Monsieur or Madame. The code, first set down in 1986, and amended in 2013, sets out the rules to be observed by police officers and gendarmes. In theory. In reality, many of the rules are ignored. Officers dealing with members of the public are routinely overfamiliar, inappropriate, aggressive in their words and actions, and insulting, and they unlawfully confiscate merchandise such as fruit and vegetables from those issued with fines.

This particular vehicle check goes off smoothly. The man riding the Vespa doesn't have his ID on him, nor does he have the vehicle registration for the moped.

The pillion passenger was smoking a joint when we stopped them. Having checked the RPF database for outstanding warrants, the Major notices that the driver has failed to appear in court pursuant to a summons. He'd been found guilty on a charge of aggravated theft, for which he'd been sentenced to twelve months. We take in the driver, leaving the passenger stranded.

Back at the commissariat, I sit with the young man while the Major writes up the report. The suspect's name is Ibrahima; he's twenty-two. I don't have to ask too many questions for him to tell me his life story:

Thing is, I've been robbing since my teens. To me it was just something you did ... I mean, I knew it was wrong. We'd steal money, phones, and other shit, rip off some guy's gold chain. When you live in Saint-Denis, that's how it goes, it's a sketchy 'hood, there's people there steal a whole lot more them me. When I first moved to Saint-Denis, I'd never stolen nothing. But I saw other guys do it, and, y'know, I kinda got into it. I lost touch with a lot of things. I didn't see my folks anymore. Every time I went back to Saint-Denis, I'd be stopped and searched. The cops would just drag me straight down the station. These days, I'm living in Paris, it's not like living on the sink estate. It's cool here, you can make a lot of connections, all that. Not gonna lie, but

I swear down, since I been livin' in the city, well,
I'm not saying I don't pull no shit any more, but
I do it a lot less.

After a number of convictions, Ibrahima has been banned from setting foot in Saint-Denis. The Major walks over, and I signal for Ibrahima to stand up. The Major is as happy as a pig in shit that he's made a good collar; he grabs the young man by the arm, and leads him over to the duty sergeant.

I go outside for a cigarette. Though I don't know it, I've just spent my last day with the Major.

49

I feel like handing in my badge to resign. I'm three-quarters of the way through what I intended would be a six-month undercover op. But, like running a marathon, the last few miles are the toughest.

In his office, my boss, Steph, is sitting behind his computer, his face glowing and tanned.

"Good holiday?" I ask.

He flashes a smile. My boss likes to focus on his family life. He favours the security of a position as Brigadier-Chef rather than taking risks out on the streets. "I tell you, in twenty years on the force, I've never chased a suspect," he confided one day.

Steph puts in the hours and never makes waves, carries out orders from the top brass, and goes home.

"In two, three years, I'll have a desk job. A cushy little number where I just tick boxes would suit me fine."

Steph is the only officer in the brigade who everyone gets along with. Probably because he doesn't bother anyone. Or maybe it's because he's an honest, decent guy.

Since the Major is on leave, Steph has taken up the baton. He'll be spending all his time in his office, managing the brigade.

"We made seventy-six arrests last month, including thirty-five on-the-spot fines," he says casually.

The thirty-five on-the-spot fines makes it possible to artificially inflate the brigade's statistics with two-bit interventions. All in all, we've racked up the numbers, but the Commandant will see the figures as lazy.

"You'll see, with these figures, I'm bound to be summoned to see the Commandant."

Steph doesn't care about the numbers. As long as he's left in peace, everything else is like water off a duck's back.

"You asked to see me …" he says.

"Can I apply for some leave? Two days, if possible, during the next cycle."

Just then, the Commissaire comes into the incident room.

"Hello," I mumble.

I'm often taken aback when I encounter her. I end up just saying a bland hello, whereas protocol requires "Good day, Madame la Commissaire". I have other senior officers I am expected to salute, including a Captain and a Commandant. I can never seem to get my head around who is who. A Captain has three stripes, and a Commandant has four. Every time I shake hands, I find myself counting the stripes. I'm completely lost.

So I just say "Hello". Even if it earns me a few funny looks.

The officers troop out of the incident room, and I find myself alone with Steph.

"So tell me, young man, which days were you thinking?"

As I formulate an answer, I think about the excuse I plan to give when I resign. I scroll through the options. A girl who lives halfway across France that I've fallen in love with. A family member who's gravely ill. No, not that, it's too close to home for me to make up something like that. Surgery? That might be the perfect excuse.

Just trying to find an excuse to resign is going to do my head in.

50

I glance at the calendar: twenty-eight days left. Seven four-day cycles. I get a text message from a girl I've been chatting to for a couple of days. We met on a dating app. When she asked what I did for a living, I told a little white lie, or maybe a medium-sized grey lie. "I am a freelance journalist." You never know — she might be a Commandant's daughter or a cop's sister. That wouldn't be good.

I stick to the rules, I try to seem funny and kind. With every week undercover, I feel a little more isolated. Aside from a couple of beers with La Merguez, a few phone calls with friends outside Paris, and a few trips to a bar to watch a football match, I've had no social life whatsoever. Since starting work at the commissariat, I've been leading a monk's life: I go to work, take notes, sleep, repeat. I spend my days off reading and chain-smoking; sometimes I pop out to buy some new books, or go for a run. The work is all-consuming, as though I never really leave the job behind.

•••

The life I used to lead seems to date back to another era. Before this — even when I was undercover — I used to go out a lot, sometimes every night. I'd drink and flirt, and sometimes I wouldn't get to bed before dawn. These moments of drunken freedom were the only times I didn't feel I was pretending to be someone else.

After another coffee and another cigarette, I half-heartedly decide to write up my recent notes. My phone screen lights up; the girl has texted back. We arrange to meet up for a drink at 9.00 pm, at a bar in Montreuil.

51

I walk faster, my headphones clamped to my ears. Julie has been waiting in front of the bar for at least ten minutes. She's twenty-nine, and other than that, I don't know much about her, besides the fact that she works in film.

She is tall, with dark, curly hair. After the usual introductions and a little small talk, I sense that I'm going to tell her what I really do for a living. We hit it off. A waiter appears at our table, and we order two pints.

Halfway through our beer, I tell her about the undercover op. At first, she's surprised, but then decides it's amazing. I feel I can trust her. She wants to know more, asks loads of questions. I tell her everything.

We go back to her place. I'd rather sleep in her bed than invite her back to mine. Living in a tiny 150-square-foot studio at the age of thirty isn't exactly impressive. Even for a journalist working undercover in the police force.

52

"Listen, I've been thinking a lot and … I'm not sure I'm going to stick it out here. I'm thinking of resigning, because …"

There: I've said it. I dared to tell a colleague that I'm thinking of resigning. This whole "model pupil" syndrome has made me dread telling people that I'm leaving. I'm afraid of disappointing, of stepping out of line, of drawing attention to myself. But it's just slipped out while I'm on sentry duty with Stan's best friend, Charly. He doesn't even let me finish the sentence.

"Hey, hey, give it time, big man. Apply to be in the regular force, and when you've got that under your belt, you can decide."

I try offering simple arguments. I talk about the days spent standing guard outside the commissariat, the fact that I'm only earning €1,340 euros a month. I tell him I can't make ends meet. Charly starts taking the piss out of me. He changes the subject, jokes about my "puny little body". I have a bit of a beer belly, and my arms look like twigs in my baggy police shirt. His biceps are three times the size of mine.

"Look at you with your glasses, you're like one of those guys on *Undercover Boss*. I bet you're really a Commissaire who's just slumming it to see how I'm doing. Then, after three or four months, you decide whether to give me a transfer. Or fire me."

If only he knew.

I remember something he once said: "I do what I like when I'm in uniform." Charly has been hauled up in front of the General Inspectorate six times on allegations of police brutality, against guys whose faces he "smashed to a pulp". In police lingo, it's referred to as "aggravated assault by a person in public authority". Charly says that's all in the past now, that he's a lot calmer these days.

As I look forward to the looming end of my undercover operation and having less weight on my shoulders, I'm worried about how my fellow officers will react when they find out who I really am.

53

Security guards at a DIY shop arrest some guy, and find batteries and some tubes of glue in his pockets. All told, the value of the stolen items comes to sixty-eight euros and change. The store manager decides to press charges, so he calls us. Our task is simply to take the shoplifter into custody. A routine job.

When we get there, Mano talks with the owner and the security guards while I check the ID of the shoplifter, a Moroccan recently arrived in France with no residence permit. In his pockets, I discover a crack pipe and a métro pass.

"Why do you think he's stealing glue?" Charly asks. "To shoot up?"

The Moroccan guy stares vacantly and says nothing. His blue baseball cap, dark tracksuit pants, and grey T-shirt are encrusted with dirt. His dark, curly hair clearly hasn't been washed in quite a while.

We don't bother with handcuffs, but sit him in the back seat of the squad car. Mano slides in next to him and nods for me to take the passenger seat.

"You didn't see anything, you didn't hear anything," Charly says.

I suddenly understand how this is going to go down. I'm riding with an officer who's boasted about "smashing faces" of prisoners in custody, and who was the officer responsible for the beating in the rue Compans.

"All good? Nobody can see us?" says Mano.

"No, no, we're all good."

Man puts the Moroccan in an arm lock and gives him a slap, and then another. He grabs the guy by the hair, and punches him hard in in the stomach. The immigrant is terrified and gasping for breath. Instinctively, he tries to grab the sleeve of Mano's shirt.

"Get your hands off me! Let go right now, or I'll break your arm!" Mano roars.

I feel deeply ashamed. But even now, I do not react. This has all gone too far. I should have got out long before now. I need to stop this. I need to end the undercover op, write about the abuse I've witnessed, publish the book, move on. I can't bear seeing any more of this violence and, worse still, being part of it.

"We're going into a tunnel, so you can really lay into him if you like," says Charly, amused. "Hey, I'd even slow down — it's not like we're in a hurry …"

"You don't steal, got that?" Mano roars, gripping the guy's elbow. The man winches in pain. Mano delivers two punches to his face.

"For a minor offence like that, the prosecutor would just send him on his way," says Charly. "He certainly wouldn't get banged up, that's for sure."

Their logic seems to be: since there's no likelihood that this guy will end up in prison, they might as well dispense justice themselves. A sentence with no trial, no paperwork, no fuss: summary justice delivered by punching him in the face. And it makes them feel good, to punch someone. Especially someone who is powerless, who will not file a complaint for police brutality, since he is an illegal immigrant.

"Where should we drop him? Pantin?" the driver asks Mano.

"Yeah, that's fine."

We come to a deserted area, and Charly pulls up, puts on the handbrake, gets out, and opens the back door.

"Right, you, get the fuck out!"

The man clambers out of the car. He can barely walk.

"My cap!" he says. "Where's my cap?"

Hearing his words, I feel sick to my stomach. I grab the cap from the back set and toss it to him.

Charly starts the car.

"Was he bleeding?" he said. "I think maybe you busted his nose, big man."

"Really? I didn't notice," Mano says defensively. "I didn't hit him that hard."

54

I step into my boss's office. It is 08:15 hours, on Friday 16 August. I take a deep breath. Last night, I rehearsed the whole speech in front of the bathroom mirror. Steph gives me a smile.

"Hey, I've been meaning to ask about your days off — do you want Christmas Day or New Year?"

"Actually, that's what I've come to talk to you about."

My voice falters, the words stick in my throat. I feel the urge to run away. Steph looks at me benevolently.

"Go on …"

"I came to talk to you … because … I want to stop."

"What do you mean, stop?"

"I want to leave the force."

"All right."

"I don't know what the process is, but I wanted to talk to you first."

"It's okay, don't worry. I'll need to look into the process. I'm sure there have been one or two since I've been working here, but I don't know the ins and outs of it."

The phone rings. Steph needs to take the call. I leave the office. Feeling sheepish. That's it. It's done.

I go down to the garage, fish a pack of cigarettes out of my pocket, and smoke one slowly.

A few minutes later, I run into Steph in the hallway.

"By the way, I didn't ask. Why do you want to quit?"

This time, my voice sounds normal. The worst is over. I can give him the spiel I'd rehearsed the night before.

"Oh, because of the salary and the assignments. I'm sick of having to drag myself out of bed at four in the morning to guard a door."

Steph nods gravely. He seems to understand.

"Assignments come from upstairs," he argues.

I continue to reel off excuses: my age, the fifteen months I spent working in the psychiatric unit. It's been too much, I've made too many sacrifices.

The following morning at 6.10 am, I sit typing at the computer. I'm resigning; it's official.

Steph takes out a pencil and a calculator. He explains that I'm entitled to seventeen days' leave. Although I have to give one month's notice, I'll be able to leave much sooner, given all the leave that I have racked up. I've got five days left to get through.

55

It is 07:45 hours, and we are at the hospital. Mano is sitting on a chair playing with his truncheon. Next door, doctors are treating a man who was stabbed twice in the arm last night. His neighbours were making a racket, so he went downstairs to complain, and ended up beaten and gassed. That's his version. There are two clear wounds. Nonetheless, he's in custody to ensure he doesn't flee.

I've got two days left. Mano shows me a video of the demonstrations in Hong Kong where officers are laying into the protesters with batons and fists, and dragging them along the ground.

"Look! Now that's real police work!" he says excitedly as he watches a man covered in blood curl into a ball to ward off more blows.

While we're hanging around waiting, I tell Mano that I've resigned. He seems surprised.

"So, what are you going to do now? Maybe you'll decide to come back. I know I could never go back to the private sector. You get guys in the force who quit and come back later."

"Maybe a few months from now, I'll realise I was stupid to quit. We'll see."

Mano tells me he used to work at Roissy Airport. He worked on the runways, but the notion of becoming a cop was always there in the back of his mind. So he applied to be an ADS, he was posted to highway patrol, and later applied to be a fully fledged officer.

"I've been in the force nearly seven years," he whispers. "I should have stayed at the airport."

"Why do you say that? I thought you liked being a cop?"

"Thing is … What kind of cop? Look, it's fine, I'm happy enough where I am."

Mano tells me Stan is planning to leave the brigade in September. He'll be posted to a BSG squad in a different area. Mano has put in for a transfer to a police action unit.

Mano launches into a torrent of abuse about our fellow officers. This guy is a "dickwad", another guy is an "arsehole", a third is "a glorified fucking social worker"; then he starts on the female officers in the brigade, who are hopeless at making arrests, "all except one".

Mano changes the subject to an incident that occurred yesterday: he filed a complaint against a prisoner in custody.

"The guy called me a filthy fucking Peruvian. So I filed a complaint. I told the whole story to the complaints officer, and he added a bunch of other stuff. He put down that I'd suffered emotional damage as a result of the guy's racist abuse. Pretty good, I thought."

56

The last day. Some guy in the custody cells has just pissed on his mattress. He was brutally assaulted on the Place de Stalingrad — his face is covered with scars and bruises. When the cops showed up, he tried starting a fight with them. So the officers gassed him. When the tear gas hit the open wounds, the guy collapsed in a heap.

Since being brought into the station, he'd been curled up in a ball on a mattress in his cell. Until he pissed himself.

Marvin holds out a roll of paper towels in his big, gloved hands.

"Here, clean it up," he says, without raising his voice. "And clean it up good."

The man does as he is told without saying a word. When he has finished, Marvin tells him to go to the bathroom and wash his hands.

"No, no, I'm not going, you'll beat me again!"

"Go on, I said." Marvin's tone is harsh now.

"Ten-SHUN!" shouts someone.

The Commissaire Divisionnaire has just shown up. I get up and stand to attention. She greets every officer, but she looks distinctly ill-at-ease.

"Good day, Madame la Commissaire," I mumble.

For once, I have managed to use the regulation greeting.

The Commissaire is in plain civilian clothes, on her way home from a leaving party. Personally, I'm not planning to celebrate tonight. I've thought about it, but I'm afraid it might seem cynical later, when they know who I really am. I'm feeling a little awkward. Not all my colleagues know that I am leaving after this shift.

The custody suite is full: eighteen prisoners in the three cells, and two drunks drying out in the other. There are three juveniles up on the third floor, all on drugs charges. One of them was carrying eight grams of hash; the other two were charged as accomplices, according to my colleagues.

I sit down again, and mentally watch sand trickle through an hourglass. Five hours and twenty-two minutes to go.

"I don't think I was cut out to be a police officer," Marvin whispers. "I've got no compassion. It's all used up. I didn't have much to start with, but now …"

It begins to dawn on me that, in the space of six months, my levels of compassion and empathy have plummeted. As though the job has inoculated me. When I started out and I first saw a victim of domestic abuse being brought into the commissariat, it sent my stress levels through the roof. Six months later, I've seen it happen so often that I don't react the same way anymore.

In the early afternoon, I get a seventeen-year-old Guinean boy to blow into a breathalyser. He was brought in earlier this morning, drunk. He had been driving. He also resisted arrest. When his blood-alcohol level drops below 0.02, he'll be moved from the drying-out cell to join the others in custody. As the day wears on, he seems to feel worse and worse. At 09:00 hours I escort him to the third floor to see the Police Judiciare.

"I've got malaria," he said. "I can't walk …"

The Guinean slumps on the bench.

"Quit faking!" a detective growls angrily. "Quit it now. You're nothing but a useless piece of shit!"

The Guinean doesn't respond. He is unconscious.

"I don't think he's faking it," I say feebly.

"Oh, he is, take my word for it," says the detective "What's your name?"

The young man's eyes are closed. He is unresponsive, so I speak for him.

"His name is Sylla. He's seventeen."

"Okay, well, he hasn't called a lawyer, he hasn't called his family. We're good here, you can put him back in the cells."

At 9.20 pm, forty minutes before I am finally free,

I drag the Guinean boy down the hall. The soles of his shoes brush the floor all the way to the cell he will be sharing with another juvenile, the kid who was caught carrying eight grams of hash.

"Listen, kid," I say, "if anything happens to this guy, I want you to warn me. Just wave your arms — I'll see you on the monitor."

I get a text from a friend: "Chin up, only a couple of minutes more."

A few minutes later, on the CCTV monitor, I see the kid with the hash waving his arms wildly. I race back and open the cell door. There is a pool of greenish liquid on the floor — the Guinean boy has just thrown up.

"It really stinks," says the kid.

The Guinean boy is lying on the ground, his head sticking out from under a pink blanket. I fetch some toilet paper and wipe away the bile. It is 9.43 pm. This is what they look like, my last moments as a cop.

Having moved the juvenile to another cell, I go back upstairs to the Police Judiciare.

"We need to call the emergency services — the Guinean kid has thrown up."

I feel like adding: "He wasn't faking, you morons!" But I bite my tongue. One last time, I bite my tongue.

At 9.53 pm, I am sitting next to Marvin, waiting for the ambulance crew to arrive. At 9.56 pm, the night shift comes on duty. The emergency services are en route.

"It's okay, big guy," Marvin says. "You can go."

•••

For the last time, I take off the navy-blue trousers, my belt, and the polo shirt emblazoned with the word POLICE. I stuff everything into my bag, pull on my civilian clothes, close my locker, and take the stairs two at a time, up to the ground floor, to the exit.

Out on the street, I walk away like a fugitive, not looking back. My brain exploding, I mentally spool through the past six months: the custody prisoners I saw being slapped on my first day; the officer from the commissariat who committed suicide; the endless racist comments and attitudes; the complaints of domestic abuse swept under the carpet; the routine insults to ordinary citizens; the general lack of respect for the public; the kid I saw being beaten up right in front of me; the fellow officer who covered for himself using false witness statements — including mine; the Moroccan immigrant beaten up in the back of the van.

Two years of my life end here. It's time to slip back into my own skin, time to tell this story.

MY THANKS

To my editors:
Clara Tellier-Savary,
Geoffrey Le Guilcher,
and Johann Zarca.

To the editorial committee and the reading committee
at La Goutte d'Or:
Alice Andersen, Franck Berteau,
Christophe Bigot, Clément Buée,
Aurélie Carpentier.

Pierre-Marie Croquet and Basile Lemaire
from les Productions de la Goutte d'Or,
Michel Despratx, Marion Enguehard,
Lucie Geffroy, Laurent Ollivon,
Camille Polloni, and Lætitia Zanettacci.

To my optician.

Valentin Gendrot

To the *eminences grises*, and those who supported me
from the shadows:
My Little Man,
My Little Man's mother,
Nikita Schwarz, Le Canariste, to Giulia,
Giulia's parents, Ahmed, Hélène,
RJ and Valedane, Édouard, my driver, Pete,
M. and Mme. Hesse, Gébé, Toto, and Doudou.

To Michel, to agent M.

NOTES

1   Camille Polloni, "'Ragheads', 'niggers', 'Jewish scum': when racist police officers speak their minds", *Mediapart*, 4 June 2020.

2   Ilham Maad, "Guardians of the peace", Arte radio, 4 June 2020.

3   Ronan Maël, "Thousands of police officers exchange racist messages on Facebook group", Streetpress, 4 June 2020.

4   *Die Welle*, a 2008 German film directed by Dennis Gansel, based on Ron Jones' social experiment "The Third Wave" and Todd Strasser's novel, *The Wave*.

5   Lucas Burel, "Assault on a student: eggs, flour and a 'police omertà' on trial", *L'Express*, 11 November 2016.

6   On 13 June 2016, Jean-Baptiste Salvaing, the commanding officer at Mureaux commissariat, and his partner, Jessica Schneider, an administration worker at the Mantes-la-Jolie police station, were stabbed to death in their home in Magnanville by Larossi Abballa, an Islamic terrorist. Abballa was later shot dead during a police raid on the house.

7   A non-governmental agency founded by Caroline de Haas fighting sexual and gender-based violence.

8 WhatsApp conversations have been transcribed verbatim.

9 Compagnie de sécurisation et d'intervention: elite police units reporting to the Central Directorate of Public Security and the Préfecture de Police in Paris, that are called out to deal with all urban violence.

10 Jérémie Gautier, "*Le contrôle au faciès devant les juges*", *La Vie des Idées*, 2 February 2018.

11 Cédric Mathiot, "Do twenty to thirty people die every year at the hands of the police?", *Libération*, 2 February 2019.

12 An independent government authority appointed by the president with a broad remit, including respect for the rights and freedoms of children, public service workers, and whistleblowers.

13 Group de Securité de proximité (Neighbourhood Support Group).

14 The Commissariat Principal (Main Police Station) refers to the Nineteenth Arrondissment Commissariat. The name dates from a time when most Paris districts had several commissariats.

15 Louise Couvelaire, "No in-depth ministerial analysis exists of suicide rates in the police force", *Le Monde*, 20 April 2019.

16 "Order concerning personal or service weapons", 9 March 2017.

17 Nicolas Bougoin, "Suicide rates in the Police Nationale", *Population*, 52, no 2, pp. 431–40.

18 Camille Polloni, "Suicides among police officers: lead in the soul", *Les Jours*, 29 April 2019.

19 Frédéric Ploquin, *La peur a changé de camp: les confessions incroyables des flics*, Albin Michel, 2018.

20 Jean-Marc Berlière and Maurice Lévy, *History of the French Police from the Ancien Regime to the Present*, Nouveau Monde Éditions, 2013, pp. 288–89.